Python Machine Learning

A Hands-On Beginner's Guide to Effectively Understand Artificial Neural Networks and Machine Learning Using Python (With Tips and Tricks)

By James Deep

Table of Contents

Introduction

We are living in a world where technology has become a primary preoccupation every day. Many industries and organizations across the universe are trying what they can so that they end up improving their production. It is because of this and other reasons that they decided to employ new techniques within the industries. New technologies, such as the introduction of Machine Learning, usage of robots, deploying of drones among others came into being. However, for many years, the rate of production in terms of data input and information output was still low. Going by this, they would look for that type of machine that could enable them to predict their outcome using the features variables that they had by then. Remember, being in a position to know the result of a specific task within the organization even before they could perform a particular task motivated them. Sadly, some types of methods used in data prediction proved to be wrong while few gave out the expected results. At one point, their data lacked enough accuracy, and some were vague, while others you could not read and interpret. Due to all these, many scientists thronged the internet and technological libraries so that they could come up with something tangible to solve the current predicament of solving the workload within the industries.

Therefore, you need to understand or comprehend why Machine Learning was the most convenient way to solve many burning issues within their labor sectors. There are several cases where human beings were only dealing with the mathematical concept of the companies' accounts in a manual way. However, this was inconvenient since many organization or industries involved huge workload that could not be done by human beings. Cases of tiredness and lack of enough knowledge to perform every task of prediction became rampant.

Therefore, Machine Learning which was fully deployed refers to a situation where some specific tasks were solved using simple algorithms and some statistical models. Machine Learning relies mostly on the inference and some patterns. To some, this is artificial intelligence while others based their belief on the mathematical models that had sample data which they later refer to as "training

2

data." The process became more manageable as this machine could make some decisions within the organization using the data available. Later on, the organization used the algorithms from machine learning to cater to the needs of the company. Up-to-date, computer vision, and even issues to do with email filtering uses algorithms from machine learning. As a result, several organizations had to realize the improved work rate, which led to high output at the end.

Many studies show that machine learning relates to some sorts of statistics, especially those from the computer. That's computational statistics. However, it is good to note that this focuses only on using computers to make much--needed decisions and predictions. Some aspects of machine learning enable it to perform its function accordingly. Examples of these are mathematical optimization which only involves application domains, uses of theory, and even different methods that make the machine learning work better. Another aspect is data mining. Many studies show that data mining relates to field study work, mainly within machine learning. Its main objective is to help in the analysis of data. In most cases, many businesses employ machine learning for predictive analytics purposes.

Chapter 1: Introduction: A Historical Overview of Machine Learning

Machine Learning came into limelight in 1959, and this happened with the help of American pioneers. Arthur Samuel, who spent much of his time in computer gaming, came up with the initial term of machine learning. During this time, machine learning became part and parcel of scientific endeavour. Later on, it widespread as the need for artificial intelligence grew. Many people, especially the researchers, got much interest in it to the extent of deploying machine learning in getting some data. At this point, the researchers had no option but to fully implement all the means at their disposal to get the required results. They ended up using perceptrons even though this was later seen as an application of linear models. Still, on this, they also deployed the probabilistic reasoning, especially in the automation of the medical diagnosis. Fortunately, this automated technique seemed to work better, thus improving their work in medical sectors.

However, issues with increased logical and an approach which depended much on knowledge caused a technological war between the Machine Learning and AI. In this juncture, you realize that the probabilistic system could not perform it's tasking as intended. That's, they had problematic issues about practical and theoretical, especially when it came to data representation and even acquisitions.

As the AI came into a great halt, the industry was left with nothing to solve their workload and heavy tasks. As a result, machine learning started flourishing again. That's, in the 1990s. It then changed its objective or goal from achieving intelligence deemed to be artificial to tackling problems mainly from practical nature. Its focus shifted. In that, the symbolic approaches came to cease. It acquired the probability theory and use of statistical models. Machine learning, later on, benefited from the digitized information and the easy way of internet distribution. Therefore, internet distribution created a transferable mode through which many scientists could use to get the machine learning. Remember, with the partial death of the AI, and Machine Learning became part and parcel of every industry. In that, many scientists and several organizations could not afford to miss it. Its usage increased as many people involved it in all kinds of data predictions.

The Evolutionary Perspective of Machine Learning

Machine learning passed through several stages to reach where it is today. The steps marked with improved technology and natural problem solving. In addition to this, the level of accuracy in output predictions increases. However, this was still below what the scientists and most organizations required. Also, the rate of solving and acquiring data became much more manageable but with few cases of inaccuracy within the output data. It is because of this that the urge to improve on the features of machine learning came to be. Therefore, all these lead to the ultimate birth of evolution.

The first stage was a game of checkers and machine learning. Here, Arthur Samuel came up with a computer program which he could use to play checkers. He induced alpha-beta pruning to cater for the less memory within the gadget. This knowledge could predict which chances of winning in the game of checkers. In the end, this resulted in a minimax algorithm. He, later on, went with his designation to improve his machine.

The next phase of evolution was the Perceptron. Frank Rosenblatt came up with this model. It was a combination of machine learning and brain cells model. It is good to note that brain cell model was the work of Donald Hebb. Frank, who used to work in the laboratory of Cornell Aeronautical, came up with this Perceptron at a time when industries were lacking ways to solve some statistical data and analysis. He planned to do his work, that's, Perceptron a machine and not anything to do with a program. Perceptron uses Mark 1 perceptron for recognition of the image. As a result, the transferring of the software and the machine became even more accessible. According to him, this was the most successful machine. Also, though this was successful, some aspects lacked solutions. That's, the device was unable to recognize visual patterns. As a result, many scientists and computers programmers went into another research. However, their struggle continues until the 1990s where they managed to come up with another problem-solving machine.

Therefore, the continued research led to the birth of another algorithm called The Nearest Neighbor.

In his work, Marcello Pelillo realized that he could easily recognize the patterns. Another main objective of this algorithm was to map routes. The usage of this program was beneficial as salespersons could use it to enter into different cities. They also used it to find the best efficient way during their day to day travel. Even though this discovery was helpful, there are some situations that it failed to tackle. As a result, it was leading to the ultimate birth of multilayers. Multilayers came into limelight in the 1960s and went ahead to improve that research of neural network. The double usage of layers increased the processing power of Perceptron, thus making it more efficient. Again, the introduction of multilayers led to the development of backpropagation. The main task of backpropagation was to solve any errors within the system. It used a principle of spreading these errors backward so that solving them may not be difficult. It is now being applied in many sectors of industry such as a neural network. It is also good to note that this system came to be in the 1970s.

Backpropagation led to the development of the Artificial Neural Network. Here, this machine could solve more complex tasks that Perceptron couldn't undertake. It involves the usage of input data which transformed into output information. The jobs here are complex, and human beings could find them difficult to tackle.

In the 1970s and some parts of 1980s, algorithms came to cease. Artificial intelligence started using logical approaches in solving its tasks. Again, there was an abandonment of some research, such as a neural network. In the end, a schism evolved between the two large bodies. That's machine learning and artificial intelligence leading to their separation. Later on, the machine learning struggled for almost ten years after its reorganization. Here, its goals moved from artificial intelligence training to provisions of services. Again, its focus led to the development of probability theories and some elements of statistics. The flourishing of machine learning came to being in the 1990s, where it was able to concentrate on the neural network. However, internet growth played a significant role in the success of this.

The next evolution involves boosting and boosting reduced bias within the data used. It deployed the use of machine learning algorithm where the transformation of weak learners into strong learners occurs. In his finding, he deduced that a set of weak learners could make one stronger learner. Machine learning has undergone many evolutions.

Examples of these evolutions may include speech recognition and much more. Therefore, it is also good to note the benefits of the machine in our daily lives.

- It helps in analyzing data, especially sales data, within the industry.

- It promotes mobile personalization

- It helps in detecting fraud

- It helps in making a recommendation about a specific product.

- It leads to proper learning management.

- It promotes dynamic pricing, thus increasing flexibility in pricing.

- It also helps in the processing of natural language. That's, you can speak with humans.

Chapter 2: Types Of Machine Learning

In a world soaked in artificial intelligence, it is interesting to understand machine learning in depth. This is a concept that allows an algorithm to perform specific tasks without relying on any explicit instructions. Instead, the machine relies on inference and patterns such that the user feeds data to a generic algorithm rather than writing the code. In response, the machine constructs the logic based on the input data. Usually, the accuracy of the prediction made by the algorithm is evaluated and the algorithm only gets deployed when the precision is acceptable.

Types of Machine Learning

There are three broad categories of machine learning. We will discuss each of them in detail below.

1. ***Supervised Learning***

   This paradigm happens to be the most popular, probably because it is easy to comprehend and execute. Here, the algorithm creates a mathematical concept from a labeled dataset, i.e a dataset containing both the input and output parameters. This dataset acts as a trainer to the model. Taking an example, we may decide to use the algorithm to determine whether a particular image contains a certain object. In this case, the dataset would comprise images with and without the input (that object), with every image having the output designating whether or not it contains the particular object. The algorithm is likely to predict any answer; whether right or wrong. However, after several attempts it gets trained on picking only the images containing the said object. Once it gets totally trained, the algorithm starts making right predictions even when new data is input. A perfect example of a supervised learning model is a support vector machine. On the diagram below, the support vector machine divides data into sections separated by a linear boundary. You realize the boundary separates the white circles from the black.

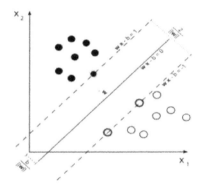

Types of Supervised Learning

- **Classification**: These algorithms are used in instances where the outputs are limited to discrete values. In the case of filtering emails for example, an incoming mail would be classified as the input, whereas the output would be the folder name.
- **Regression**: This is the algorithm under which the output has a continuous value, which means they many pick on any value within a given range. Perfect examples include; temperature, wind speed, price of a commodity etc.

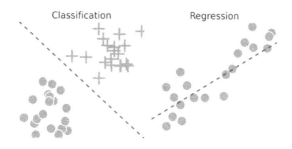

Supervised machine learning is exhibited in many common applications, some of which we have discussed below.

> **Advertisement Status**: Most of the ads that you encounter when browsing the internet are positioned there because a supervised learning algorithm vouched for their clickability and popularity.
> **Face Recognition**: This one is quite common on Facebook. It is very likely that your face has been used in a supervised algorithm that is trained to recognize it. When Facebook is suggesting a tag you must have noted that the system guesses the persons on the photo, which is a supervised process.
> **Spam Classification**: The spam filter that you find on your modern email system is a supervised learning concept. Apart from preemptively filtering spiteful emails, the system also allows the user to provide new labels and express their preference. See the illustration on the figure below.

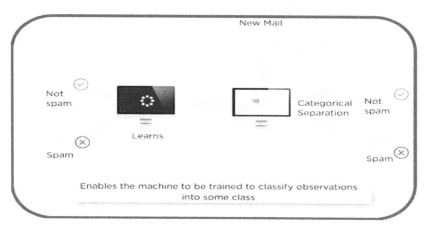

2. *Unsupervised Learning*

As the name suggests, unsupervised machine learning is the exact opposite of supervised learning. The model finds structures in the data and also learns through observation. When given a dataset, the model automatically finds relationships and patterns by creating clusters in the dataset. The paradigm cannot add labels to the created cluster, but it does the creation perfectly. This means that if we have a set of apples and oranges, the model will separate the apples from the oranges, but will not say that this is a set of oranges or apples.

Now, suppose we had more than two sets, say we present images of grapes, oranges, and apples. As explained above, the model, based on some relationships and patterns, will create clusters and separate the datasets into those clusters. Whenever new data is input, the model adds it to one of the already built clusters as shown in the figure below. You realize the output is grouped perfectly even without addition of labels.

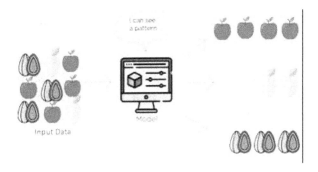

Let us take another classical example for better understanding. Think of a little baby and his family dog. He very well identifies its features. When a family friend brings along another dog to try play with the baby, the baby will identify that as a dog even without anyone telling them. They will easily classify it because it has the features like two eyes, ears, walks on four, among other details. This falls under unsupervised learning because you classify the input data without being taught. If it were supervised learning, the family friend would have to tell the baby that it's a dog.

11

Types of Unsupervised Learning

- **Clustering:** This concept identifies a pattern in an assortment of unclassified data. Clustering algorithms categorize any existing natural groups in the data. The user is also at liberty to adjust the number of cluster they want their algorithms to identify. Under clustering there are more types that you can utilize;

  ❖ **Exclusive (partitioning)**
  Under this type, classification of data is done such that one data can only belong to a single only. K-means serves as a perfect example.

  ❖ **Agglomerative**
  This is the technique where every data is in itself a group. The number of clusters is reduced by the iterative mergers between the two closest groups. An example is the hierarchical clustering.

  ❖ **Overlapping**
  Under this technique, data is associated with a suitable association value. Fuzzy sets are used in grouping data and each point could fit into two or more groups with different membership degrees. Fuzzy C-Means is a suitable example under this type.

  ❖ **Probabilistic**
  This concept creates clusters using probability distribution. See the example below given some keywords;

    o "Men's pants"
    o "Ladies' pants"
    o "Men's wallets"
    o "Ladies' wallets"

  The given keywords could be grouped into two; "pants" and "wallets" or "Men" and "Ladies".

- **Association**

  The rules under association allow the user to institute associations in the midst of data objects inside big databases. As the name suggests, the technique seeks to discover unique relations between variables contained in large databases. For instance, shoppers could be grouped based on their search and purchase histories.

Applications of Unsupervised Machine Learning

Unsupervised ML is based on data and its attributes, and Therefore, we can conclude that it is data-driven. The results from a task are controlled by the nature in which the data is formatted. Some of the common areas that rely on unsupervised learning include but are not limited to;

➢ **Buying Habits:** It is not surprising to find your purchasing habits stored in a database somewhere. The information could be used by marketers to group clients into similar shopping segments so that they can reach out to them easily. The clustering is easy to do under unsupervised learning algorithms.

➢ **Recommender Systems:** If you are a Netflix or YouTube user you might have encountered a video recommendation severally. Often times these systems are contained in the unsupervised domain. The system knows the watch history of its users. The model uses the history to identify relationships between users who enjoy watching videos of certain genres, length, etc, and prompt them with a suggestion of related videos that they may not have watched.

➢ **Identification of Fraudulent transactions:** Anomaly detection is the technique used in discovery of abnormal data points. The algorithm picks out any unusual points within the data set, hence sending an alarm.

Supervised Vs. Unsupervised ML Techniques

Data specialists employ an array of machine algorithms in their discovery operations. Below are some insights on the classification of supervised and unsupervised learning techniques, which will help you to judge when to use either of the techniques.

Parameters	Supervised machine learning	Unsupervised machine learning
Data usage	Employs training data to study the link between the input and output.	Does not use output data.
Accuracy of the outcome	Highly accurate reliable.	Less accurate and Therefore, not trustworthy
Input data	Labeled data is used in training the algorithms.	Algorithms are used against unlabeled data.
Number of classes	Known number of classes.	Unknown number of classes.
Major drawback	Classification of big data.	Failure to get precise information concerning output and data sorting due to use of labeled and unknown data.
Real time learning	Learning takes place offline.	Learning happens in real time.
Process	Both input and output variables are given.	Only the input data is given.
Computational complexity	Relatively simple; less complex.	Complex in terms of computation.

Deciding to employ a supervised or unsupervised machine learning algorithm classically depends on your data volume and structure.

Essentially, a well-formed data science plan will employ both algorithm types to come up with predictive data models. Now, these models are more advanced and help the stakeholders in decision-making across a variety of business hold ups.

3. *Reinforcement Learning*

This is a neural network learning technique that trains machine learning concepts how to make a progression of decisions. The agent is trained how to attain their objective in an indecisive, potentially complex environment. In this technique, an artificial intelligence engages into a game-like situation and the computer tries to solve the problem using trial and error method. For the programmer to get the machine to do what they want, the artificial intelligence gets penalized or rewarded for the actions performed. The idea is to fully exploit the total reward.

Usually there is a reward policy in form of game rules, but the designer does not give any hints on how the model should solve the puzzle. The model starts from completely random trials and advances to sophisticated approaches and even superhuman skills. In the process, this technique leverages the full power of search, hence qualifying to be the most effectual in hinting machine's creativity. As opposed to humans, artificial intelligence can employ a reinforcement algorithm to collect experience from thousands parallel gameplays as long as it is run on an adequately powerful computer infrastructure.

Let us look at a practical example that will perfectly illustrate the reinforcement learning technique. However, before then we need to understand some terms that we will use in the illustration.

- **Agent:** This is an implicit entity that seeks to gain a reward by performing actions in an environment.
- **Environment (e):** A situation that an agent must face.
- **Reward (R):** An instant response given to an agent on performing a specific action.
- **State (s):** The current scenario returned by the environment.

- **Policy (π):** An approach employed by the agent to determine their next action based on the prevailing state.
- **Value (V):** The projected long-term return, which is discounted comparing with the short-lived reward.
- **Value Function:** This one stipulates the total reward, i.e, the value of a state.
- **Model based methods:** Handles the reinforcement learning-based problems that apply model-based techniques.
- **Model of the environment:** It imitates the behavior of the environment, helping you draw conclusions regarding environment behavior.
- **Action value / Q value (Q):** This is not very different from value. In fact, the only variation is that this one takes an extra parameter as a current action.

Illustration

Think of trying to teach your dog some new tricks. This dog does not understand human language so you need to devise a strategy that will help you achieve your goal. You will initiate a situation and observe the various reactions by your dog. If the dog responds in the desired way, you give him some beef. You will realize that every time you expose the dog to a similar condition, they will tend to respond with greater enthusiasm hoping to get a reward (the beef). It means that the positive experiences inspire the responses your dog gives. As well, there are the negative experiences that teach the dog what not to do because should they do it, then they will certainly miss their share of beef.

In the given paradigm, your dog is an agent exposed to the environment. You may decide to have your situation as requiring your sitting dog to walk when you utter a particular word. This agent responds by performing an action where they transition from one state to another, like transitioning from sitting to walking. In this case, the policy is a process of choosing an action given a state with the expectation of better results. After transitioning, the agent may get a penalty or a reward in response.

Reinforcement Learning Algorithms

There are three techniques in implementation of a reinforcement learning algorithm.

i. **Value-based:** here, the agent is anticipating a long-term return of the prevailing states under policy and so you ought to maximize the value function.

ii. **Policy-based:** under this RL scheme you endeavor to find a policy such that the action executed in each state leads to maximal reward in the future.

Policy-based method is further classified into deterministic, where the policy produces the same action for any state, and stochastic, where every action has a definite probability determined by the stochastic policy. The stochastic policy is n{a\s} = P\A, = a\S, =S]

iii. **Model-based:** in this case you are expected to generate a virtual model for every environment, where the agent learns how to perform in that very environment.

Types of Reinforcement Learning

i. Positive

This is an event triggered by specific behavior. It positively influences the action taken by the agent. This happens through enhancing the frequency and strength of the behavior. This method helps you to capitalize on performance and sustain change for a longer period. Even so, you have to be careful as over-reinforcement may cause state over-optimization and impinge on the results.

ii. Negative

It involves strengthening behavior prompted by a negative condition which should have been dodged or stopped. Although it helps define the least stand performance, this method provides adequate to meet up the minimum behavior, which is a drawback.

Applications of RL in Real Life

- ➢ Data processing and machine learning.
- ➢ Planning of business strategy.
- ➢ Robotics for industrial computerization.
- ➢ Aircraft and robot motion management.
- ➢ Helps in creation of customized training systems for students.

Summary

- Data used in unsupervised learning is labeled and unknown, and Therefore, you cannot get accurate information concerning data sorting.
- When moving from image to image you will have varied information because the spectral properties of classes are also likely to change over time.
- Unsupervised machine learning locates all unknown types of unidentified patterns in the data.
- The user has to dedicate time to label and interpret the classes which follow a particular classification.
- The major downside of unsupervised learning is the failure to get accurate information in regard to data sorting.
- Reinforcement learning is a machine learning method with three algorithms; 1) value-based, 2) policy-based and 3) model based.
- The two types of reinforcement learning are 1) positive and 2) negative.
- RL should not be used for problem-solving when you have adequate data.
- The major RL method drawback is that learning speed may be affected by parameters.

Chapter 3: Use of Python in Machine Learning

Machine learning and associated technologies such as artificial intelligence (AI) are the technologies for the present and future. In a world that is increasingly aggregated towards more personalized gadgets and machines with improved and technical functionalities, tech companies and innovators are on the overdrive, researching, developing and testing the innovative technologies of the future. These technologies are aimed at revolutionizing the human experience while also cementing the place of machines especially computers as the primary drivers of all spheres of human life. While seemingly dedicated to meeting the ever-changing human demand technology and hence, user experience, these companies and individuals are also seeking to develop technologies that can increase their bottom line. These new technologies not only use huge of data to execute complex processes that cannot be accomplished manually, they are also come with increased accuracy and efficiency. They can also analyze data patterns to make predictions and come with solutions to problems beforehand. Essentially, machine learning and AI are premised on turning the numerous scientific fictions of the past decades into reality.

However, AI technology comes with the added disadvantage of collecting and analyzing large volume of data to process in order to execute these complex processes. Additionally, bringing science fiction to life also require skill sets in programming, creativity, conceptualization, ideation, and analysis. But most importantly, it requires the right programming language that is easier to understand and flexible to work with. The last thing you need as a programmer writing the algorithms for the next game changer technology that would transform human experiences is being stack with a programming language that is inflexible and incapable of handling data complexity. This can easily lead to error in the coding of the machine's program or applications. A code error can lead to embarrassing situations for developers as exemplified in the 2016 case involving Microsoft's chat box which malfunctioned and resorted to communicating misogynistic messages to the millennials instead of the intended happy and positive themed messages. Amazon, the world's leading online retailer also suffered a reputational damage in 2014 when its AI machine designed for talent recruitment turned in a discriminative tool that singled out female applicants. These are just a few cases involving well-established tech giants whose Machine Learning and AI algorithms were erratic due programming issues.

Python and AI and ML

Training a computer to possess human-like ability of learning and making predictions without continuous specific process-based programming can be daunting task without the right programming language. By eliminating the need for explicit programming, a program developer would then need to feed the computer the right training data what the computer will use as a point of reference, more like a library to learn from. This is one of the primary points of departures between traditional and non-traditional programming projects such as IA or machine learning. Using the training data, a programmer will be able to develop a software using numerous lines of codes to create the desired algorithms for the machine. However, such complex project require a mastery of statistics and mathematical optimization to achieve the best result: an algorithm free of coding errors which can lead to machine malfunctioning. Additionally, a programmer should also understand the concept of probability to

20

ensure that the developed algorithms are capable of making predictions which one of the primary functional capabilities of machines equipped with AI capabilities.

To facilitate the execution of such complex programming tasks, Python, a programming language conceived by the software engineering guru Guido van Rossum, is equipped with various libraries or modules. These modules come in handy for programmers when coding as they have inbuilt code pieces that are already written. Programmers can use these pre-written codes as the backbone of the algorithms they are aiming to write for a specific project. With a pre-existing code, a programmer has the jumpstart to develop even complex algorithms that artificial intelligence-based technologies require. This is because the codes that comes with the programming language modules have level items that support basic functionalities. They also act as launch pads for the next set of coding actions thereby eliminating the need for starting afresh any programming project.

Python's extensive library ecosystem includes: Scikit-learn, Seaborn, NumPy, and Pandas. Others include Keras and SciPy. These sets of library are specialized for different tasks during the development of algorithms for AI and machine learning. For example, Seaborn module is primarily used for coding tasks involving visualization of training data to be used in machine learning. This includes exploration of data with the view of plotting statistical patterns. It is from these patterns that machines use their AI to project scenarios.

On the other hand, Pandas is readily the most popular set of library among programmers using Python language because of its functional versatility. The module is suitable for all forms of coding-related data analysis. As an object-oriented language, Python relies heavily on analysis and interpretation of these data during coding to develop algorithms that the machine can learn from and use the knowledge to make predictions. This is why SciPy and NumPy are the most important Python libraries. The bulk of Python programming-related projects use these two libraries. NumPy lacks the general-purpose nature of Pandas even though it is also used for analyzing coding data. However, it is most suitable in analyzing high-performance data.

Scikit-learn library is the most flexible of all these modules and plays an important role in the overall simplicity, flexibility, and versatility of

Python as a programming language. It can be easily integrated with other modules such as NumPy and SciPy to achieve greater coding success. Programmers using Scikit-learn library will find it easy to implement tasks during coding as this will take only a few lines to accomplish. Such functional simplicity in task implementation is because Scikit-learn is compatible with unsupervised and supervised algorithms, a variety in algorithms that machine learning and AI rely on to achieve functional autonomy. Therefore, coding that involves probability testing, mathematical optimization and statistics such as regressions, decision trees, and k-means are easily executed using Scikit-learn library set.

Basics of Using Python Modules in Machine Learning Projects

The first step towards developing algorithms for your machine learning project using Python programming language is problem identification. Programming for machine learning is a targeted undertaking aimed at tackling a specific problem. Therefore, when fully defined, a problem will help the programmer in developing the parameters of the algorithm and the data set to be collected. Defining a problem directs the whole coding process. It will determine what kind of predictions that machine will be able to make as well as identifying its functional integrity. That is, identifying the integrity of the algorithm and the program used by the machine.

Secondly, determine whether your version comes with or without prebundled modules. Python's anaconda and miniconda packages usually come with the fundamental module: SciPy Libraries. Upon installation, SciPy libraries come with preinstalled modules such as NumPy, Scikit-learn, Pandas and SciPy among others. In case the Python package does not come with SciPy libraries, download the library and instill it. For prebundled packages, use the cmd command and type the specific name of the module to install. Always make sure that your versions of the bundles are updated. Using the latest version of modules will allow the programmer to access new and better features that improves the integrity of their software or applications.

After installing and updating Python and the modules, import all the relevant objects and modules that will be required during the coding process. The type of libraries imported is dependent on the dataset and the functional capability that the algorithms are projected to achieve. This should be followed by loading the dataset to be used for machine learning from the relevant source suing the Pandas modules. The loaded training data should be prepared appropriately to meet the project needs. It should be large enough to improve the accuracy of the predictions of the machine. Adding randomness links to your training dataset will improve the machine's ability to make predictions. In case you are using a hosted version of the dataset due unreliability issues, it is always advisable to include a link to it. This will reduce cases of coding errors as a result of using redundant dataset.

A dataset summary will give the programmer insights on his or her dataset dimensions including classes and attributes such as number of data columns. Additionally, it shows a brief overview of the dataset. A programmer also has the chance to discern the various statistical attributes associated with the data they are using for coding. After summarizing, it is advisable to visualize the dataset using either univariate or multivariate plots. Plotting allows a programmer to have a greater understating of the relationships between the various variables within the dataset to be used in developing algorithms for the machine. Data visualization is done using Pandas libraries which has different options for visualization including scatterplots and distribution graphs. Testing the dataset using models and a validation dataset before developing the final algorithms for machine learning is very important. Validation dataset will act as your point of references whenever you are using the algorithms to predict unseen dataset. Moreover, it also act as a starting for any further changes and improvements you will need to make on the algorithms; it eliminates the need to start all over again in case of coding error.

Benefits of Using Python in M.L. and A.I.

One of the reasons behind Python's growing popularity as a programming language of choice for many programmers is its relatively large library ecosystem. Python's library ecosystem is comprised of numerous modules and extensions that support the implementation of a wide range of coding tasks including data analysis and visualization among others. From Pandas to SciPy, NumPy and Keras, Python has a wide range of libraries that gives it the versatility needed to code even for complex algorithms.

It also boasts of simple syntaxes and semantics that are easy to follow and use. They have a math-like characters which make them easier to familiarize with when coding. This makes coding with Python easier and less technical. Mastering basic coding using Python does not require technical knowhow. This makes coding preferable among basic users as opposed to other mainstream programming languages such as Java and C. It is also a general-purpose language that makes it easy to use to developing a wide range of algorithms for machine learning.

Summary

The past few decades has been marked by a radical transformation in the tech world with new inventions being churned out from production conveyor belts of individual and corporate entities. The dawn of a new era marked by complex machines and megadata is upon us. Machines equipped with artificial intelligence are increasingly being incorporated into almost all spheres of human life. These machines are capable of high performance and execution of very technical and complex tasks that are impossible to complete manually. They also achieve such performances with a high level of accuracy and autonomy from human. This is the era of artificial intelligence and machine learning. Despite the apparent maturity and age of machine learning, it's perhaps the best time to learn it, primarily because of its practical uses. And Python is probably the best programming language that can help you excel in your career in this field. With a robust understanding of fundamental machine learning and Python skills, you should be all set to dive deeper. Just remember the fact that as with learning any skill, the more you work with it, the better you become. Practicing with diverse types of algorithms and trying to work with different datasets obtains a solid understanding of machine learning using Python, and enhances your overall problem-solving skills in event space.

Chapter 4: Essential Libraries For ML In Python

Many developers nowadays prefer the usage of python in their data analysis. Python is not only applied in data analysis but also statistical techniques. Scientists, especially the ones dealing with data, also prefer using python in data integration. That's the integration of Webb apps and other environment productions.

The features of python have helped scientists to use it in machine learning. Examples of these qualities include consistent syntax, being flexible and even having a shorter time in development. It also has that ability to develop sophisticated models and has engines that could help in predictions.

As a result, python boasts of having a series or set of very extensive libraries. Remember, libraries refer to a series of routines and sorts of functions with different languages. Therefore, a robust library can lead to tackling of more complex tasks. However, this is possible without writing several code lines again. It is good to note that machine learning relies majorly on mathematics. That's mathematical optimization, elements of probability and also statistical data. Therefore, python comes in with a rich knowledge of performing complex tasks without much involvement.

The following are examples of essential libraries being used in our present.

Scikit – Learn

Scikit learn is one of the best and a trendy library in machine learning. It has that ability to supporting learning algorithms, especially the unsupervised and supervised ones.

Examples of Scikit learn include the following.

- ❖ k-means
- ❖ decision trees
- ❖ linear and logistic regressions and also
- ❖ clustering

This kind of library has major components from NumPy and SciPy. Scikit learn has the power to add algorithms sets which are useful in machine learning and also tasks related to data mining. That's, it helps in classification, clustering, and even regression analysis. There are also other tasks that this library can efficiently deliver. A good example includes ensemble methods, feature selection, and more so, data transformation. It is good to understand that the pioneers or experts can easily apply this if at all, they can be able to implement the complex and sophisticated parts of the algorithms.

TensorFlow

It is a form of algorithm which involves deep learning. They are not always necessary, but one good thing about them is their ability to give out correct results when done right. It will also enable you to run your data in a CPU or GPU. That's, you can write data in the python program, compile it then run it on your central processing unit. Therefore, this gives you an easy time in performing your analysis. Again, there is no need for having these pieces of information written at C++ or instead of other levels such as CUDA.

TensorFlow uses nodes, especially the multi-layered ones. The nodes perform several tasks within the system, which include employing networks such as artificial neutral, training, and even set up a high volume of datasets. Several search engines such as Google depend on this type of library. One main application of this is the identification of objects. Again, it helps in different Apps which deal with the recognition of voice.

Theano

Theano too forms a significant part of python library. Its vital tasks here are to help with anything related to numerical computation. We can also relate it to NumPy. It plays other roles such as;

- ❖ Definition of mathematical expressions
- ❖ Assists in the optimization of mathematical calculation
- ❖ Promotes the evaluation of expressions related to numerical analysis.

The main objective of Theano is to give out efficient results. It is a more fast python library as it can perform calculations of intensive data up to 100 times. Therefore, it is good to note that Theano works best with GPU as compared to the CPU of a computer. In most industries, the CEO and other personnel use theano for deep learning. Also, they use it for computing complex and sophisticated tasks. All these became possible due to its processing speed. Due to the expansion of industries with a high demand for data computation techniques, many people are opting for the latest version of this library. Remember, the latest one came to limelight some years back. The new version of Theano, that's, version 1.0.0, had several improvements, interface changes and composed of new features.

Pandas

Pandas is a library which is very popular and helps in the provisions of data structures which are of high level and quality. The data provided here is simple and easy to use. Again, it's intuitive. It is composed of various sophisticated inbuilt methods which make it capable of performing tasks such as grouping and timing analysis. Another function is that it helps in a combination of data and also offering filtering options. Pandas can collect data from other sources such as Excel, CSV, and even SQL databases. It also can manipulate the collected data to undertake its operational roles within the industries. Pandas consist of two structures that enable it to perform its functions correctly. That's Series which has only one dimensional and data frames which boast of two dimensional. Pandas has been regarded as the most strong and powerful python library over the time being. Its main function is to help in data manipulation. Also, it has the power to export or import a wide range of data. It is applicable in various sectors, such as in the field of data science.

Pandas is effective in the following areas:

- ❖ Splitting of data
- ❖ Merging of two or more types of data
- ❖ Aggregating of data
- ❖ Selecting or subsetting of data and
- ❖ Data reshaping.

Diagrammatic explanations
Series Dimensional
SERIES

A	7
B	8
C	9
D	3
E	6
F	9

Data Frames dimensional
DATA FRAME

	A	B	C	D
*0	0	0	0	0
*1	7	8	9	3
*2	14	16	18	6
*3	21	24	27	9
*4	28	32	36	12
*5	35	40	45	15

Applications of pandas in a real-life situation will enable you to perform the following:

28

❖ You can quickly delete some columns or even add some texts found within the Dataframe
❖ It will help you in data conversion
❖ Pandas can reassure you of getting the misplaced or missing data
❖ It has a powerful ability, especially in the grouping of other programs according to their functionality.

Matplotlib

This is another sophisticated and helpful data analysis technique that helps in data visualization. Its main objective is to advise the industry where it stands using the various inputs. You will realize that your production goals are meaningless when you fail to share them with different stakeholders. To perform this, Matplotlib comes in handy with the types of computation analysis required. Therefore, it is the only python library that every scientist, especially the ones dealing with data prefers. This type of library has good looks when it comes to graphics and images. More so, many prefer using it in creating various graphs for data analyzation. However, the technological world has completely changed with new advanced libraries flooding the industry. It is also flexible, and due to this, you are capable of making several graphs that you may need. It only requires a few commands to perform this.

In this python library, you can create various diverse graphs, charts of all kinds, several histograms, and even scatterplots. You can also make non- Cartesian charts too using the same principle.

Diagrammatic explanations

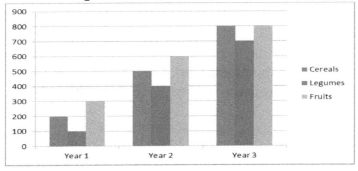

The above graph highlights the overall production of a company within three years. It specifically demonstrates the usage of Matplotlib in data analysis. By looking at the diagram, you will realize that the production was high as compared to the other two years. Again, the company tends to perform in the production of fruits since it was leading in both year 1 and 2 with a tie in year 3. From the figure, you realize that your work of presentation, representation and even analyzation has been made easier as a result of using this library. This python library will eventually enable you to come up with good graphics images, accurate data and much more. With the help of this python library, you will be able to note down the year your production was high, thus, being in a position to maintain the high productivity season.

It is good to note that this library can export graphics and can change these graphics into PDF, GIF, and so on. In summary on this library, the following tasks can be undertaken with much ease. They include:

❖ Formation of line plots
❖ Scattering of plots
❖ Creations of beautiful bar charts and building up of histograms
❖ Application of various pie charts within the industry
❖ Stemming the schemes for data analysis and computations
❖ Being bin a position to follow up contours plots
❖ Usage of spectrograms and lastly
❖ Quiver plots creation.

Seaborn

Seaborn is also among the popular libraries within the python category. Its main objective here is to help in visualization. It is important to note that this library borrows its foundation from Matplotlib. Due to its higher level, it is capable in various plots generation such as the production of heat maps, processing of violin plots and also helping in generation of time series plots.

Diagrammatic Illustrations

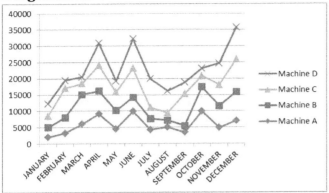

The above line graph clearly shows the performance of different machines the company is using. Following the diagram above, you can eventually deduce and make a conclusion on which machines the company can keep using to get the maximum yield. In most occasions, this evaluation method by the help of seaborn library will enable you to predict the exact abilities of your different inputs. Again, this information can actually help for future reference in the case of purchasing more machines. Seaborn library also has the power to detect the performance of other variable inputs within the company. For example, the number of workers within the company can be easily identified with their corresponding working rate.

NumPy

This is a very widely used python library. Its features enable it to perform multidimensional array processing. Also, it helps in the matrix processing. However, these are only possible with the help of an extensive collection of mathematical functions. It is important to note that this python library is highly useful in solving the most significant computations within the scientific sector. Again, NumPy is also applicable in areas such as linear algebra, derivation of random number abilities used within industries and more so Fourier transformation. NumPy is also used by other high-end python libraries such as TensorFlow for Tensors manipulation. In short, NumPy is mainly for calculations and data storage. You can also export or load data to Python since it has those features that enable it to perform these functions. It is also good to note that this python library is also known as numerical python.

SciPy

This is among the most popular library used in our industries today. It boasts of comprising of different modules which are applicable in the optimization sector of data analysis. It also plays a significant role in integration, linear algebra, and other forms of mathematical statistics. In many cases, it plays a vital role in image manipulation. Manipulation of the image is a process that's widely applicable in day to day activities. Cases of photoshops and much more are examples of SciPy. Again, many organizations prefer SciPy in their image manipulation, especially the pictures used for presentation. For instance, wildlife society can come up with the description of a cat then manipulate it using different colours to suit their project. Below is an example that can help you understand this in a more straightforward way.

The first picture above is an original image of a cat which the wildlife society took.

The above refers to the second picture, which has undergone manipulation. It is a tinted image of a cat. When you resize this image according to your preference, you will come up with the picture below.

Keras

This is also part and parcel of python library, especially within machine learning. It's also joining the group of networks with high level neural. It is significant to note that Keras has the capability of working over other libraries, especially TensorFlow and even Theano. Also, it can operate nonstop without mechanical failure. In addition to this, it seems to work better on both the GPU and CPU. For most beginners in the python programming, Keras offers a secure pathway towards their ultimate understanding. They will be in a position to design the network and even to build it. Its ability to prototype faster and more quickly makes it the best python library among the learners.

PyTorch

This is another accessible but open source kind of python library. As a result of its name, it boasts of having extensive choices when it comes to tools. It is also applicable in areas where we have computer vision. Computer vision and visual display play an essential role in several types of research. Again, it aids in the processing of Natural Language. More so, PyTorch has the abilities to undertake some technical tasks that are for developers. That's enormous calculations and data analysis using computations. It can also help in graph creation which mainly used for computational purposes. Since it is an open-source python library, it can work or perform tasks on other libraries such as Tensors. In combination with Tensors GPU, its acceleration will increase.

Scrapy

Scrapy is another library used for creating crawling programs. That's spider bots and much more. The spider bots frequently help in the data retrieval purposes and also applicable in the formation of URLs used in the web. From the beginning, it was to assist in data scrapping. However, this has undergone several evolutions and led to the expansions of its general purpose. Therefore, the main task of the scrappy library in our present-day is to act as crawlers for general use. The library led to the promotion of general usage, application of universal codes, and so on.

Statsmodels

Statsmodel is a library with the aim of data exploration using several methods of statistical computations and data assertions. It has many features such as result statistics and even characteristic feature. It can undertake this role by the help of the various models such as linear regression, multiple estimators, and analysis involving time series, and even using more linear models. Also, other models, such as discrete choice are applicable here.

Chapter 5: Regression Analysis (Linear Regression and Logistic Regression)

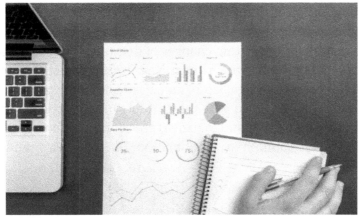

Several industries across the globe are struggling with the best way to come up with the correct data or information that will eventually enable them to solve their incurring prediction problems. Several banks have made some losses, especially within their credit section as they could not correctly predict the trustfulness of the defaulters. In the health sector, you realize many have lost their lives because of poor planning and risk management, which come as a result of the lack of modeling to tool for more straightforward prediction. We also have other sectors such as weather forecasting where farmers were not advised on the occurrence of rain, as a result leading to more losses. Another area involved the payment of mortgage by homeowners. Due to all these, everyone across the universe went on a rampage looking for the best possible way to handle the prediction roles of the organizations. Later on, all these gave birth to what is termed as regression analysis.

Therefore, regression analysis refers to statistical processes for prediction analysis using variables. In that, it helps in identifying the variables relationships. This analysis consists of both independent and dependent variables. In other words, regression analysis aids in understanding the effect of one independent variable on the dependent variable when other independent variables are kept constant. In most cases, regression analysis will try hard to predict the conditional expectation, especially of the variable which is dependent. Regression analysis is applied in several areas such as weather forecasting and prediction. Here, it helps predict the outcome of the rain within a specific period. It is also applicable in other fields such as medical sectors for predicting chances of diseases. Regression analysis comprises of the following: linear regression, logistic regression, polynomial, stepwise, ridge, lasso, and elastic net regression. All in all, this chapter will only tackle the most widely used regression analysis, such as linear regression and logistic regression. It is good to note that ElasticNet regression is a combination of the Lasso and Ridge regression.

Logistics Regression

Logistic regression comprises of logistic model, logistic function, statistics model, and much more. Therefore, many organizations apply logistic regression in their day to day activities which mainly composed of data predictions and analysis. You can always conduct this regression analysis, especially when the dependent variable is binary. That's dichotomous.

Just like other types of regression analyses, logistic regression is entirely applied in any analysis dealing with prediction. Its primary function, in this case, is to describe data. Also, logistic regression can be used to explain or illustrate the kind of relationship between the binary variable, which is dependent and the rest variables which are independent. In some occasion, this regression might look challenging to interpret, but by the help of the logistic tools such as Intellectus Statistics, you can easily undertake your data analysis.

Logistic regression knowledge can be easily applied in statistics by the help of the logistic model. In this case, the primary function of the logistic model is actually to come up with the correct results of certain predictions or class by the help of probability. For example, probability works best in areas where you are only required to predict the outcome of the existing events. These events include: healthy or sick, win or lose, alive or dead, or even in places where you are making your analysis about the test where someone either fails or pass. Still, in this model, you will be able to fine-tune your result primarily through probability. In the case of an image, you will be able to extend your model to cover up various classes. You will be able to detect whether the image in your analysis is for a lion or a cat, and so on. In this case, the individual variable within the image will have their probability number between 0 and 1. However, the sum here should be adding up to one.

Therefore, logistic regression refers to a basic statistical model which makes greater use of the available logistic function regardless of the complexity of more extensions that might exist. Logistic regression is part and parcel of the regression analysis, and on many occasions, it is applied in various analyses where logistic model parameters are estimated. Remember, the logistic model is like a form or a type of binary regression. Therefore, a binary regression consists of a binary logistic model. This model is composed of a dependent variable which includes of two possible values of events. These values can be represented as pass/fail, alive/dead, good/bad, and much more. You need to note that the indicator variable actually denotes these possible values and always they have labeled 0 and 1. Within this logistic model, the odds logarithm that's log-odds, for the values of 1 represents a linear combination. In that, this combination has got one or more variables which are entirely independent. In this case, they are called predictors here.

Moreover, in logistic regression analysis, independent variables sometimes may each form a binary variable or sometimes a continuous variable. In the case of a binary variable, there must be the presence of two classes or event, and they have to be coded by the indicator variables. However, on the other hand, continuous variable represents real value. In the logistic regression analysis, the corresponding probability of these values always varies between 0 and 1 as has been denoted previously above. In this analysis, these log-odds, that's, algorithms of odds will be converted by logistic function into probability. Log odds are measured in logit which also a derivative of its name (logistic unit). Again, you can also use a probit model with a different sigmoid function to convert the log odds into a probability for easy analysis. You need to note that the probit model is an example of an analogous model which comprises of the sigmoid function.

All in all, you will realize that the logistic model is the most preferred in this conversion due to its defining attributes or characteristics. One such feature of the logistic model is its ability to increase the multiplicatively scales of each of the independent variables. As a result of this, it produces an outcome with parameters assigned to each independent variable at a constant rate. However, this will generalize the odd ratio if at all, it is part of a variable which is a binary dependent. It is also good to note that there are extensions when it comes to dependent variables, especially in some regression such as binary logistic. However, this extension is only applicable where two or more levels are used. These two extensions include multinomial logistic regression which works best with categorical outputs, especially the one having several values that's, two values and above. The next type of logistic regression extension is the ordinal logistic regression which deals with a huge collection of multiple categories. A good example here is the ordinal logistic model dealing with the proportional odds. However, this system only does modeling and not performing any classifications dealing with the statistics since it is not a classifier. Therefore, it will only convert the probability input into an output. Following this, let us discuss the applications of logistic regression in a real-life situation.

Now that we have had a chance to take a look at what this logistic regression is all about, we are going to take a look at some of the steps that we can take to write one of our own in the Python language. There are other languages that we can use with data analysis and these algorithms, but we are going to focus on the Python language because it comes with the libraries that we talked about earlier, and it is an easy one to work with.

In general, a binary logistic regression is going to help us to describe what relationship, if any, is going to be present between our dependent variable, which should be binary, and one or more of the independent variables. When we work with the binary dependent, there are two outcomes that are possible for the dependent variable. 1 is going to be used for success or true, and then 0 will be for failure or false. There are a few steps that need to happen here in order to get the process to work in the manner that we want. We will look at the code in a moment, but first, let's talk about a few of the parts that are there. We need to gather the data that we want. There is usually a dataset that will help us with this. You can create your own, or you can import one that is already created to help.

Then we need to import some of the packages that are needed to make this code work. For this code, we are going to make sure that we have seaborn, sklearn, and pandas on our computer. If these are not already installed on your system, then take the time to do this because we need them. When the libraries and packages are all ready to go, it is time for us to build up our data frame, This is usually going to be something that we are able to do with the Pandas library, but you can choose the method that works the best. And that is where we are going to move on to creating the logistic regression with the Python language.

When we are ready to bring all of these parts together, we can then write out the code. The code to help us with this is below:

```
import pandas as pd

from sklearn.model_selection import train_test_split

from sklearn.linear_model import LogisticRegression

candidates = {'gmat': [780,750,690,710,680,730,690,720,740,690,610,690,710,680,770,610,580,650,540,590,620,600,550,550,570,670,660,580,650,660,640,620,660,660,680,650,670,580,590,690],

    'gpa': [4,3.9,3.3,3.7,3.9,3.7,2.3,3.3,3.3,3.3,1.7,2.7,3.7,3.7,3.3,3.3,3.3,2.7,3.7,2.7,2.3,3.3,2,2.3,2.7,3.3,3.7,2.3,3.7,3.3,3,2.7,4,3.3,3.3,2.3,2.7,3.3,1.7,3.7],
```

'work_experience':
[3,4,3,5,4,6,1,4,5,1,3,5,6,4,3,1,4,6,2,3,2,1,4,1,2,6,4,2,6,5,1,2,4,6,5,1,2,1,
4,5],

'admitted':
[1,1,1,1,1,1,0,1,1,0,0,1,1,1,1,0,0,1,0,0,0,0,0,0,1,1,0,1,1,0,0,1,1,1,0,0,0,0,
1]

}

df = pd.DataFrame(candidates,columns= ['gmat',
'gpa','work_experience','admitted'])

X = df[['gmat', 'gpa','work_experience']]

y = df['admitted']

X_train,X_test,y_train,y_test =
train_test_split(X,y,test_size=0.25,random_state=0) #in this case,
you may choose to set the test_size=0. You should get the same
prediction here

logistic_regression= LogisticRegression()

logistic_regression.fit(X_train,y_train)

new_candidates = {'gmat': [590,740,680,610,710],

'gpa': [2,3.7,3.3,2.3,3],

'work_experience': [3,4,6,1,5]

}

df2 = pd.DataFrame(new_candidates,columns= ['gmat',
'gpa','work_experience'])

y_pred=logistic_regression.predict(df2)

print (df2)

print (y_pred)

Applications of Logistic Regression

Logistic regression is applied in metrological and other forecasting stations which consist of meteorologists. The algorithm here is used to predict the probability of rain. This information is vital as it helps in many sectors such as agricultural, transport and so on. Time of planting can efficiently be planned for, and the right arrangement can be put into place. This analysis is also applied in some risk management systems such as credit control system. Here, the analysis will predict whether the account holder is a defaulter when it comes to payment or not. Still, on this, the regression analysis will predict the exact amount that someone can be given by using the previous records. This always enables many organizations to run, as they are able to control everything when it comes to risk management. All accounts will undergo a critical analysis before any credit is appended. Logistic regression is also applied in political sectors, especially during an election. Here, it gives out the probability of winning and losing each candidate owing to their strengths and resources they used. Again, this regression analysis will be able to predict the number of people who might fail to vote and who will vote at the end and to which particular candidate. Some factors help determine the prediction outcome here such as the age of the candidate, sex, the incomes of both the candidate and the voters, state of the residence of both and more so, total number of votes in the last elections.

Logistic regression is also applied in various medical fields. It is applied in epidemiology. Here, the analysis is used to identify all those risk factors that may eventually result in diseases. As a result, precautions and other preventive measures may be put into place. Its knowledge is usable in the Trauma and Injury Severity Score(TRISS) where predictions of mortality, especially in injured patients, are done. We have several medical scales which have been designed to check on the severity of patients across the globe.

All these medical scales have been developed or managed using logistic regression. In most cases, especially within the health sector, you can use this knowledge to predict the risk of acquiring some dangerous diseases. For examples, diseases such as coronary heart disease, diabetes, and other forms of health-related complications can be easily controlled. These predictions are based on the day to day observable characteristics of the individual patient. The traits or characteristics here include the body mass index, sex, age, and even different results of their blood tests. This will eventually help in proper planning and risk management in the medical sector.

Again, this knowledge can be applied in the engineering sector. Here, it is used to predict the failure probability of a particular system, a new product, or even any kind of process. In the field of marketing, logistic regression analysis helps to determine the buyers' purchasing power, their propensity to purchase, and also this knowledge can be used to stop the various subscriptions of the companies. The technique is also applied in economics. Here, knowledge is used to predict the outcome of being involved in the public labor sector. We also have this technique in the issues to do with the probability of homeownersnot paying a mortgage. Natural language processing uses conditional random fields which is also an extension of logistic regression, especially to sequential data.

Logistic Regression vs. Linear Regression

You may be wondering about the main difference between these two examples of regressions. In terms of the outcome, linear regression is responsible for the continuous prediction while there is a discrete outcome in logistic regression. A model predicting the price of a car will depend on various parameters like color, year of make, and so on. Therefore, this value will always be different, indicating the continuous outcome. However, a discrete outcome is always one thing. That's, in case of sickness, you can either be sick or not.

Advantages of logistic regression

- It is very effective and efficient

- You can get an outcome without large computational resources

- You can easily interpret it

➤ No input features required for scaling process

➤ No tuning required

➤ You can easily regularize logistic regression

Linear Regression

Linear regression refers to a statistical approach used for modeling a relationship between various variables in a particular set of different independent variables. In this chapter, you'll learn more about dependent variables such as response as well as independent variables, including features of simplicity. To be able to offer extensive search results and have a clear understanding regarding linear regression in python, you need to be keen on the primary basis. We begin with the primary version of the subject. For instance, what it is a simple linear regression?

By definition, simple linear regression refers to a significant approach that's used in predicting a significant response by utilizing a single feature. Therefore, it's assumed that the main two variables, in this case, are directly related. That's why it's vital to determine the linear function since it often predicts the main response value of the equation accurately. There are different regression models utilized in showing as well as predicting the main relationship between two different variables as well as factors. As such, it's important to note that the main factor that's being predicted is known as the dependent variable. But the factors utilized in predicting the main value of the dependent variable is identified as the independent variable. With that said, it's also vital to note that good data doesn't always narrate the entire story as it may be. Therefore, regression analysis is often used in the research as well as the establishment of the correlation of variables. However, correlation isn't the same as the subject of causation. Therefore, a line found in a simple linear regression which may be fitting into the data points appropriately may not indicate a definitive element regarding a major cause and effect relationship. When it comes to linear regression, every observation has two values. Therefore, one of the values is specifically for the dependent variable. The other is certainly for the independent variable.

Linear Regression in Python

Linear regression refers to a statistical approach used for modeling relationship between various variables in a particular set of different independent variables. In this chapter, you'll learn more about dependent variables such as response as well as independent variables including features of simplicity. To be able to offer extensive search results and have a clear understanding regarding linear regression in python, you need to be keen on the primary basics. Linear regression is also defined as linearity found in algebra. It often refers to a unique linear relationship found between two as well as more variables. Drawing from the said relationship, the result becomes a straight line. For that reason, we begin with the primary version of the subject. For instance what is simple linear regression?

By definition, simple linear regression refers to a major approach that's used in predicting a significant response by utilizing a single feature. Therefore, it's assumed that the main two variables in this case are directly related. That's why it's vital to determine the linear function since it often predicts the main response value of the equation accurately. There are different regression models utilized in showing as well as predicting the main relationship between two different variables as well as factors. As such, it's important to note that the main factor that's being predicted is known as the dependent variable. But the factors utilized in predicting the main value of the dependent variable is identified as the independent variable. With that said, it's also vital to note that good data doesn't always narrate the entire story as it may be. Therefore, regression analysis is often used in the research as well as establishment of the correlation of variables. However, correlation isn't the same as the subject of causation.

Therefore, a line found in a simple linear regression which may be fitting into the data points appropriately may not indicate a definitive element regarding a major cause and effect relationship. When it comes to linear regression, every observation has two values. Therefore, one of the values is specifically for the dependent variable. The other is certainly for the independent variable. When discussing the simple linear regression analysis, we are looking at some of the simplest forms of regression analysis that are used on various independent variables as well as one independent variable.

Consequently, in such a model, a straight line is often used in approximating the main relationship between an independent as well as dependent variable. Multiple regression analysis occurs when there are 2 major independent variables applied in regression analysis. As a result, the model is not going to be a slightly simple linear one. Usually, this model $(y= \beta o +\beta 1 + E.)$ *represents simple linear regression.* By applying the relevant mathematical convention, two main factors are herein involved. They include x and y which are the main designations. Also, the equation often provides a description on how y correlates with x. This is what is defined as the regression model. Apart from that, the linear regression model has an error term which is often represented by E. It can also be termed as the Greek letter epsilon. Usually, this error term is applied to mainly account for the variability found in y. However, this element cannot be explained in terms of the linear relationship found between x as well as y. It's also important to note that there are parameters representing the major population being studied. Some of these parameters represent the main population that is being studied. Usually, a regression line can easily show how a unique positive linear relationship, no relationship, as well as a negative relationship.

With that said, if the line that has been graphed appears to be in a simple linear regression that's flat in any way, there is no relationship that will be found in the two variables. On the other hand, if the regression line slopes upwards with the line's lower end located at y, on the graph, then there will be a positive linear relationship within the graph. But if the regression line tends to slope downward where the upper end of y that intercepts at the graph's axis. In the case where the parameters are well identified and known, the equation of the simple linear regression can utilize the computed meaning of the value of y. But in real practice, there are various parameter values that aren't known. Therefore, they have to be estimated using some form of data sample from the actual population. Therefore, the parameters of these populations are often estimated using sample statistics. These statistics can be represented using bo + b1.

It's evident that we are living a world that requires us to use tons of data coupled with powerful computers as well as artificial intelligence. While this may only be the beginning, there is a rise in use of data science in various sectors across the world. Machine learning is also driving image recognition as well as autonomous vehicles development and decisions based in the sector of finance as well as energy industry. As such, linear regression in python is still a fundamental statistical as well as machine learning technique. Therefore, for those who aspire to do statistics or scientific computing, there are high chances that this will be a requirement in the course work. Not only is it advisable to indulge in the learning process but also proceed to various complex methods appended to the studies.

It's important to understand the different types of linear regression. One of them includes multiple linear regressions which involves a unique case of the linear regression that has two to more independent variables. As such, in a case where there are two independent variables, it happens that the probable regression function is going to represent a major regression plane situated in a three-dimensional space. As such, the objective of the regression appears to be the value that will determine different weights. This also happens to be as close to the actual response as possible. In a different scenario, the case that exceeds two independent variables is often similar.

However, it's general more general as well. In a similar case, you may regard polynomial regression as a major generalized issue of linear regression in python. With that said, you can easily assume the polynomial dependence found between the output as well as inputs. In that case, your regression function may also be f which can include other non-linear terms. Usually, linear regression is the initial machine learning algorithm that data scientists encounter in their practice. It's a vital model that everyone in the sector should master. This is because it helps in laying a strong foundation for different machine learning algorithms. Since this is a powerful technique that can be applied in different sectors as discussed in the earlier chapters, it becomes important for professionals in scientific sectors to grasp the basis of using the subject. For starters, it may be utilized in forecasting sales by analyzing sales data for initial months. Also, it may be used in gaining important insight regarding consumer behavior.

Now that we have had some time to talk about how we can work with the linear regression and how it is going to work, we need to take this a bit further and look at some of the coding that we can write out to work with this. Again, we are going to stick with the Python language. And since we are looking at a graph to see how things are going to work and where our points will end up, we need to work with not only the NumPy library, but also the matplotlib library as well. The code that we need to use in order to make our own linear regression work includes the following:

```
import numpy as np

import matplotlib.pyplot as plt

def estimate_coef(x, y):


  # number of observations/points

  n = np.size(x)


  # mean of x and y vector

  m_x, m_y = np.mean(x), np.mean(y)


  # calculating cross-deviation and deviation about x

  SS_xy = np.sum(y*x) - n*m_y*m_x

  SS_xx = np.sum(x*x) - n*m_x*m_x
```

```python
    # calculating regression coefficients
    b_1 = SS_xy / SS_xx
    b_0 = m_y - b_1*m_x

    return(b_0, b_1)
def plot_regression_line(x, y, b):

    # plotting the actual points as scatter plot
    plt.scatter(x, y, color = "m",
            marker = "o", s = 30)

    # predicted response vector
    y_pred = b[0] + b[1]*x

    # plotting the regression line
    plt.plot(x, y_pred, color = "g")

    # putting labels
    plt.xlabel('x')
    plt.ylabel('y')
```

```python
# function to show plot
    plt.show()
def main():

    # observations
    x = np.array([0, 1, 2, 3, 4, 5, 6, 7, 8, 9])
    y = np.array([1, 3, 2, 5, 7, 8, 8, 9, 10, 12])

    # estimating coefficients
    b = estimate_coef(x, y)
    print("Estimated coefficients:\nb_0 = {} \
        \nb_1 = {}".format(b[0], b[1]))

    # plotting regression line
    plot_regression_line(x, y, b)
if __name__ == "__main__":
    main()
```

Take some time to look through this code, and add it to your compiler to see how it is going to work for your needs. You may be surprised at how well it works and all of the neat things that you are able to do with this code along the way. And with that, you are done creating your first linear regression!

Chapter 6: The Perceptron

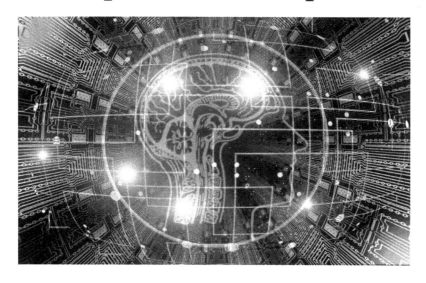

This chapter is set to look at the perceptron learning algorithm, which was first applied and propose by Minsky. This chapter offers explicit coverage of perceptron as an algorithm rather than the model. I would advise my readers to find reference material for the same topic in my book *MACHINE LEARNING FOR BEGINNERS*. In the book, the coverage of this topic is limited in scope. However, in this one, I offer an in-depth analysis of perceptron based on the content, structure, and applicability.

Defining Perceptron

A perceptron is a layer of the neural network that is capable of doing the following.

Configuring arithmetic values to the core of the data pool and estimating the sum of the positive return to the value of 1 for positive (+) outcomes.

In a different point of view, a perceptron can also be considered as a model for computation that draws a boundary (a line in two-dimensional cases) to isolate two classes in a given space.

Initially, the weights and the bias which represents the classification hyperplane is usually unknown. In this case, unsystematic weights and bias are allocated to the model. The random assignment leads to misclassification of points.

The Perceptron Trick

The objective of the perception trick is decreasing the amount of misclassified points. The reduction can be made by sliding the line over the space. In other words, it is altering the expression of the hyperplane. For all the wrongly categorized points, we adjust the weights and prejudice to move the hyperplane closer to the points that are improperly classified. After some time, the algorithm will rectify the problem to classify the points correctly. However, in this chapter, I choose to look at the perceptron differently. The approach taken is to identify perceptron in the context of the machine learning algorithm. Here, the perceptron is defined as an algorithm that predicts whether a given feature belongs to a specific class or not. From this angle, the algorithm is considered a binary classifier that is used for supervised machine learning. In most cases, the feature to be studied is always represented by a number with both magnitude and direction. As a classifier, the perceptron is used for linear classification and representation of data in graphical forms. The graphical representation model can take either two-dimension or the multi-dimension way. The perceptron identifies a feature, weighs its sum, and give an outcome of value that is 1 if the weighted summation is higher than the result from other function. The equation supports this statement in the image below

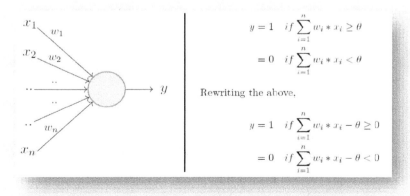

$$y = 1 \quad if \sum_{i=1}^{n} w_i * x_i \geq \theta$$

$$= 0 \quad if \sum_{i=1}^{n} w_i * x_i < \theta$$

Rewriting the above,

$$y = 1 \quad if \sum_{i=1}^{n} w_i * x_i - \theta \geq 0$$

$$= 0 \quad if \sum_{i=1}^{n} w_i * x_i - \theta < 0$$

When the equation edge is substituted (second equation in the image above) and made to be constant with the weight of a given parameter, the equation in the image below is arrived at.

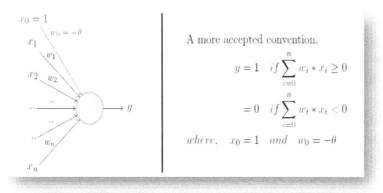

A single unit of a perceptron algorithm can be used to perform a divisible linear equation. The only group works by weighting or assigning a weight to both Boolean and positive metrics, with a corresponding partiality.

Using a Perceptron to Perform an OR Function

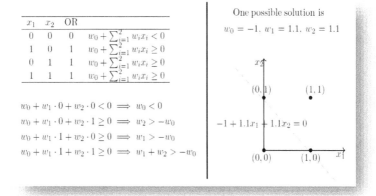

In the image above, conditions have been defined in line with the OR function. Such terms are meant to meet the optimum model, which requires the summation of weighted data to be zero (0) or more than it, for a given outcome of value one (1). The summations of the weights have been done a straight line that separates the positive (+) values from negative (-) values established.

The Minsky proposal set out the standards of learning the features by the use of sample data. The proposed models have been described below.

Basic Components of Linear Algebra

Vector

The vector value can represent a lot of things depending on the type of data and the user. Thus, there is more than one way of describing a vector. It may be a feature in space with both directing and magnitude, a structure or a database used to keep large amounts of data, etc. for this study; we will look at a vector as a line with an arrow being the head and the other point without an arrow as the origin. This is not the best definition. However, I want you to just grab the end. The images used in this presentation are mined from 3Blue1Brown.

Representing a Vector

A vector can be expressed in a two-dimension and a three-dimension plane, depending on the choice of the user and the function. Below is a two-dimensionally described vector(the first image) and a 3-D one (the second image.

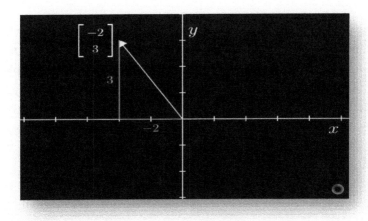

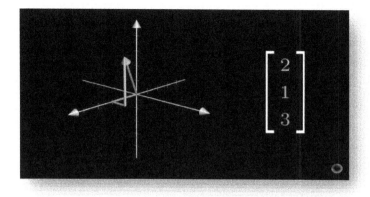

Calculating the Dot Product of Two Vectors

Given two vectors (n+1, w) and (n+1, x), their dot product is calculated using the formula below. For substitution of value, the formula I written in a matrix form.

$$\mathbf{w} = [w_0, w_1, w_2, ..., w_n]$$
$$\mathbf{x} = [1, x_1, x_2, ..., x_n]$$
$$\mathbf{w} \cdot \mathbf{x} = \mathbf{w}^{\mathrm{T}}\mathbf{x} = \sum_{i=0}^{n} w_i * x_i$$

From the equation, the vectors /w/ and /x/ are represented by a line with an arrow. The dimension of the vectors is the (n+1) value. The outcome of the computation represents the dot product of vectors /w/ and /x/. This result shows the extent to which a single vector goes to the direction of the other vector. A perceptron creates a line that separates the positive value from the negative ones. This line is called the separating boundary. For the function in our example, this is represented as, w. x = 0.

The Angle Between Two Vectors

The dot product mentioned above can be calculated using a different method. However, certain conditions must be met

I.   The angle between the vectors must be known.
II.   The magnitude of the vectors must be known.

When conditions are met, the computation of the dot product is done by substituting in the formula in the image below.

$$\mathbf{w}^T\mathbf{x} = \|\mathbf{w}\|\|\mathbf{x}\|\cos\alpha$$

The reverse method can be used to determine the angle between the two vectors. This can be done by first identifying the vector, getting its magnitude and the dot product.

The image below can guide in the substitution of values into the equation.

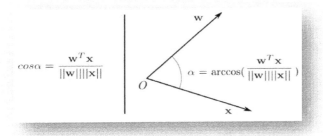

From the equation and a mathematical point of view, we know that when the cosine of an angle is 0, then the lines making the angle are perpendicular to each other. Taking from this, we can conclude that when the dot product of vectors /w/ and /x/ is 0, then line w is perpendicular to line x. that is the relationship between the dot product and the angle between two vectors.

Problem Representation Using the Perceptron

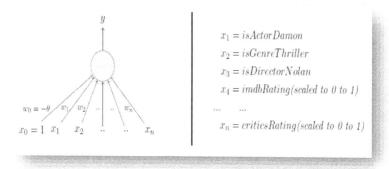

$x_1 = isActorDamon$

$x_2 = isGenreThriller$

$x_3 = isDirectorNolan$

$x_4 = imdbRating (scaled\ to\ 0\ to\ 1)$

$x_n = criticsRating (scaled\ to\ 0\ to\ 1)$

The set example is going to be used to determine if a person will settle on a movie, basing on previous data and inputs that are indicated on the diagram. The input data provided in this diagram have both real (+) and negative values (-). The actual values represent the movies watched by the person in question. We will use the data to see how the perceptron learning algorithm estimates weight in a dataset. For simplicity and clear visualization, we are going to use a 2-D representation.

Using the Perceptron Learning Algorithm

The main objective here is identifying the vector that can separate the real (+) from the negative (-) inputs, say vector (w), as used in the example.

We will use the set algorithm below.

```
Algorithm: Perceptron Learning Algorithm
P ← inputs   with   label   1;
N ← inputs   with   label   0;
Initialize w randomly;
while !convergence do
    Pick random x ∈ P ∪ N ;
    if x ∈ P   and   w.x < 0 then
    |   w = w + x ;
    end
    if x ∈ N   and   w.x ≥ 0 then
    |   w = w − x ;
    end
end
//the algorithm converges when all the
  inputs are classified correctly
```

The first step is adjusting the vector (w) with any other vector. After the initialization, we restate the examples provided in the dataset, in this instance, the metrics are P, U, and N. the examples represent both real and negative standards.

Proceeding the substitution phase, an input x (randomly picked vector) corresponds to the value P, the dot product to be determined in w, x should be stated as a value that is either equal to zero (0) or greater than zero. The actual value is not actually, outstanding since the perceptron will only give a yes or no answer.

In another instance, when vector x corresponds to the value N, the calculated dot product gives a zero (0) outcome. The statements above can be represented in one IF situation in a while loop as;

```
while !convergence do
    Pick random x ∈ P ∪ N :
    if x ⊂ P    and    w.x < 0 then
        w = w + x :
    end
    if x ∈ N    and    w.x ≥ 0 then
        w = w − x :
    end
end
```

The deduction from these representations can give two outcomes

The first outcome is when vector x corresponds to the P-value, and the dot product of the two vectors (w, x) is less than zero (w.x < 0).

The second outcome is found when the vector x corresponds to the value of N, and the dot product of the two vectors (w, x) is more significant than zero (w.x>0).

Note that we have to update the w value that has been initialized. In other cases, we are not supposed to mess the value of w, since the two outcomes above are in contradiction with the perceptron rule. For the first outcome, we will summate w and x whereas for the secondary outcome we will deduct the value of x from w.

Assessing the Viability of the Update Rule Above

The basic rule of perceptron has helped us to determine that vector x corresponds to the value P. Therefore,; the remaining part of the task is making the equation to be w.x > 0. The equation can also be interpreted to mean that when vector x corresponds to P, then the angle between the two vectors (w, x) is supposed to be less than ninetydegrees. Why this inference? The cosine of the angle between the two vectors (w,x) is the same as the dot product of the two vectors. Thereby, that angle should be less than ninety degrees.

$$cos\alpha = \frac{\mathbf{w}^T\mathbf{x}}{||\mathbf{w}||||\mathbf{x}||} \quad \bigg| \quad cos\alpha \propto \mathbf{w}^T\mathbf{x}$$

$$\text{So if } \mathbf{w}^T\mathbf{x} > 0 \quad \Rightarrow cos\alpha > 0 \quad \Rightarrow \alpha < 90$$

$$\text{Similarly, if } \mathbf{w}^T\mathbf{x} < 0 \quad \Rightarrow cos\alpha < 0 \quad \Rightarrow \alpha > 90$$

From the above interpretation, we get that we don't have to know the vector w given that it makes an angle that is less than ninety degrees with a given feature vector. In this case, the vector must be a positive value. On the other hand, vector w should make an angle that is greater than ninety degrees with a feature vector that has a negative value. This represented, as shown below.

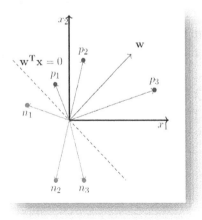

At this point, we can comfortably say that the angle between vectors x and w should be a value less than ninety, for the given case that x corresponds to the value of P.

In the same way, we can conclude that the angle made between vectors w and x should be a value that is more than ninety degrees for a given condition that the vector x corresponds to the value of N.

Moving forward, we take a look at why the update worked. The diagram below presents the explanation as to why the upgrade works. The valuation may be a bit way-out, but the general picture is seen.

(α_{new}) when $\mathbf{w_{new}} = \mathbf{w} + \mathbf{x}$	(α_{new}) when $\mathbf{w_{new}} = \mathbf{w} - \mathbf{x}$
$cos(\alpha_{new}) \propto \mathbf{w_{new}}^T \mathbf{x}$	$cos(\alpha_{new}) \propto \mathbf{w_{new}}^T \mathbf{x}$
$\propto (\mathbf{w} + \mathbf{x})^T \mathbf{x}$	$\propto (\mathbf{w} - \mathbf{x})^T \mathbf{x}$
$\propto \mathbf{w}^T \mathbf{x} + \mathbf{x}^T \mathbf{x}$	$\propto \mathbf{w}^T \mathbf{x} - \mathbf{x}^T \mathbf{x}$
$\propto cos\alpha + \mathbf{x}^T \mathbf{x}$	$\propto cos\alpha - \mathbf{x}^T \mathbf{x}$
$cos(\alpha_{new}) > cos\alpha$	$cos(\alpha_{new}) < cos\alpha$

For the case that vector x corresponds to P, we will have to add the values of vectors x and w. the addition raises the cosine of (alpha) function. This also means that the value of alpha is reduced (which is the angle between two vectors). The diagram below indicates how we can learn the vector w, which meets with a real object to make an angle that is less than ninety degrees and an angle greater than ninety degrees with negative-value objects.

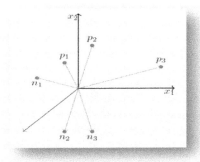

Proof of Convergence

There is no precise explanation to make people believe that the vector studied will converge in the end. This is due to the varying conditions within different sets of data. Even though it looks that there might be cases where the vector fails to converge, the truth is that the algorithm is proven to converge at some point. Many types of research have studied the patterns and deduced these proofs. Videos demonstrating this can be found in YouTube and other platforms.

Summary

In this chapter, I have taken a look at the perceptron algorithm, defined it, and went on to illustrate how it works. In so doing, I have refreshed your minds on the necessary components of linear algebra before proceeding to study the perceptron learning algorithm. This step by step presentation is meant to guide learners in understanding and visualizing the concept of machine learning, taking note of the perceptron. It is my wish that by the end of the chapter, you have gained insight and knowledge to get you started. Additional materials of study are recommended.

Chapter 7: Useful Platforms For Python Programming

Python is ported in several platforms to enable secure access. These platforms have improved over the years to become sophisticated and specialized for users. Useful platforms for Python programming include AIX, ISO, OS, VMS, and PH-UX. Other platforms for Python programming are Cygwin, Java, FreeBSD, Java, OpenBSD, Solaris, and Windows. Python 3 and 2 can be downloaded for AIX for free. Machine learning forms an integral part of artificial intelligence and helps businesses to discover information from run predictions and data. Data scientist writes machine learning algorithms to help users learn data trends. Moreover, it is used to make predictions beyond basic analysis. Other tools used for simple analysis do not make predictions, thereby making work difficult. Therefore, using these platforms for Python programming makes work easy. Python is a programming language used to write machine learning algorithms. It is used by many because of its applicability and simplicity. Moreover, packages written in Python help data scientists perform data visualization, model building, data analysis, and feature extraction. AIX users are free to use machine learning packages to perform data mining, scientific computation, and data analysis. Because the packages are based on Python, users must install the latest version of

Python on their AIX systems. They can use YUM to install AIX. It is better to use YUM because it is the easiest way out. Furthermore, it is the fastest way to install an open-source RPM package because you do not need skills to use it. You can download YUM from AIX toolbox repository and install it on AIX. The good thing about this process is that Python2 will be installed by default. Ensure that you update all the packages after installing YUM. To install machine learning packages, users need specific open source packages. These include blas, lapack, gcc, xz, python3, and zeromq. There are additional settings that are required to complete a machine learning package installation. Users need to increase resource limits for successful installation. The data and stack limits should also be increased. There are several web applications that enable users to write code for statistical analysis, and analysis. Jupyter Notebook is one of them and it does an excellent job. To facilitate the installation process, AIX users should use Jupyter Notebook to write data analysis models. To install the Jupyter Notebook, users should run this command: # python3 -m pip install jupyter. In case you do not have it in your folder, run this command, # jupyter notebook - generate-config. Python machine learning tools have gained popularity among data scientists. Moreover, AIX users want these packages on AIX to help them write AI applications. AI applications are demanding and these platforms make it easier to get things into perspective.

Linux is common among geeks and programmers. This operating system is fantastic for everyone, including students. What most people do not know is that Linux is also great for programming. There are numerous reasons why people should consider using Linux for programming. The first great thing about Linux is that it is free. Users do not incur any cost to download and install Linux on their computers. This means that it can be used by anyone, especially those facing financial difficulties, but still want to use a good Python platform. It does not matter whether you are a hobbyist or take programming as a career. The only important bit is that you don't incur any cost to use Linux operating system. The only thing that you need is a Linux compatible machine and chances are that you already have it. Moreover, most of the software that comes with Linux is free, reducing the cost of operation further. This means that you can pick the tools that you want without worrying about extra expenses. Another added advantage of using Linux is the fact that it is easy to install. Many people never get to install an operating system because they do not understand how it works or its significance. The good thing about using Linux is that it is easy to install. Some people think that since it is difficult to install other OS that it is the same case with Linux, but that is far from the truth. A programmer can easily know how to search for a Linux OS and proceed to install it. There is no difficulty pressing the function key and following the prompts. After booting a live USB drive, installing Linux becomes similar to installing a program in windows. Users who want to keep current OS can do so by choosing the dual-boot option. Another reason why you should use Linux for python programming is because it creates time to improve your skills. It is easy to access the source code and in any part of the OS. While it is difficult to use, it allows you to dive in and learn how it works. Furthermore, users are not worried about legal woes when they make mistakes. Linux offers support for programming languages to facilitate learning. It supports CSS, Java, HTML, and C++ and other languages one might be interested in. Operating languages that are not limited to specific operating systems work fine on Linux. In case a language you desire to use is not installed by default, you can get them from the distribution's repository. Linux users have the freedom to choose from a wide range of applications. The common image of a programmer is sitting in from a machine full of green or white texts. Linux offers many tools that programmers can use to have an easy time. It also allows users to pick IDEs or integrated desktop environments. Users also get to experience the power of bash scripting and apply it to python programming. Most of the commands in Linux are extremely powerful which enable users to live in the terminal. Bash script enable users to put commands together to create complex combinations. Many people long to have Linux expertise and the great way to learn it is by using in in Python programming.

Windows is a great platform for Python programming. The first thing you need to do to use Windows for Python is to set up the development environment. For those who are new to Python, it is ideal

63

for getting Python from the Microsoft Store for installation. It utilizes basic Python3 interpreter and comes in handy in an educational environment. In case you are using Python on Windows for web development, create a development environment. Instead it directly on Windows, install Python through the Windows Subsystem for Linux. Installing Python from the Microsoft Store is easy. Press the start bar, and key in Microsoft Store and click the link to open it. Choose search and type 'Python' which will open Python 3.7. When Python has finished the download and installation process, use the start menu to open Windows PowerShell. Pip is part of the Microsoft Store installation process. You can use VS to install visual studio code. Make use of the IntelliSense to facilitate the process. You can also use linting to avoid making errors. Visual studio code comes with a built-in terminal to help you open the Python command line. Download VS Code for windows to install it. To run a Python code, you need to guide VS Code which interpreter to employ. To be on the safe side, use Python 3.7 unless you have a different reason for using something different. Open the Command Palette to select Python 3. Type the command python and choose the command Python. Once you select the interpreter, select the command. The Select Python environment shows a list of interpreters that can be used. Select 'view' to open the terminal in VS Code. Enter the command to open Python in the VS Code. You can decide to install Git or not. For those who plan on collaborating with others on the Python code, VS Code enables this control via Git. You need to download and install Git for windows. An install wizard will ask a series of questions, and it is best that you use default settings. The web installer is an initial download which download components automatically. Two options are given after starting the installer; install now and customize installation. If you choose to install now, it will not be mandatory for you to be an administrator. Moreover, Python will be installed in the user directory, and shortcuts will be limited to current users. On the other hand, if you select 'customize the installation,' you will be able to choose features to install and where to install. Customize installation enables all-users installation, although users are required to prove administrative authority. Furthermore, Python is downloaded in the file directory, and there are optional features to choose from. Available options in the installer UI can be listed from the command line. It is possible to set up these options without interfering with the UI to change some defaults. Users can pass the /quiet option to hide the installer UI. This option also enables them to install Python silently.

Another platform that is useful for python programming is Java. Most Java programmers who make a move to Python find it difficult to handle its object-oriented approach. The truth of the matter is that the approach taken by Python to work with objects and language abilities and that of Java are different. This makes switching between languages hectic and confusing. Java classes are put in files using the same name of the class. Object-oriented languages keep data concerning the object. Data is stored in attributes for Python and Java.

The most notable difference between Java and Python, how classes are defined and managed. It is important to note that some of the issues faced are imposed by the languages. One is supposed to outline attributes in the class when using Java. The number one rule is that you must define class attributes before using it. On the contrary, Python requires users to define and define attributes. You can opt to create instance variables, but it is not a good idea as it leads to confusion. Moreover, you are supposed to declare variables outside a method when dealing with Python. Java is the one that has access to attributes and methods by stipulating the difference between private and public data. Attributes are expected to be private in Java to limit access to them from outside the class. In case you forget to specify the access level, the attribute defaults to package safety to limit access. However, it is not advisable to declare public attributed in Java. One is supposed to declare private attributes but use public access techniques. Whenever Python sees attributes with double underscores, it fixes things by writing the original name using an underscore.

Python and Java have numerous similarities. Both have strong support from cross-platforms and extensive standard libraries. Furthermore, they treat things as objects, compile to bytecode, although Python is compiled at runtime. Both form part of the Algol family, but it is not a must to provide a type whenever someone declares an array in Python. Static type is known for catching type errors during compilation. Therefore, using Java helps to catch a mistake if you did not want to mix integers and strings. Static typing made code run regardless of whether it eliminates errors. Whitespace forms an important part of Python syntax. The declaration creates a block in each case. It not clear whether Python's typing is better than Java, but using them both maximize results. Users who use Python for Java programming benefit greatly. Java has better performance than Python, and incorporating it into programming improves the process. Java has no tuple, an immutable collection of values. Python is used by many because it has a high speed, and is reliable and efficient. It is also dynamic and has an elegant syntax. Users do not need to compile the program before executing it.

The OS module present in Python allows interaction with the OS. OS is a Python standard and offers a portable alternative of employing OS dependent functions. It has many functions that enable interaction with the file system. Functions in OS are many, such as OS name, which gives the name of the operating system module imported. Names registered under this are 'posix' 'java,' and 'nt.' Different interpreters have different outputs. OS also enables the getcwd function, which returns the current working directory to execute the code. OS error is a function of the OS which invalid file names that are not accepted by the OS. OS popen opens a pipe to a command can be read if the mode is 'r' or 'w.' OS module allow users to interface with the OS that is run on by Python. OS is preferred because it returns the actual process ID and information that identify the current operating system. It also allows users to change the root directory when they want to. It returns entries to file directory and names it. It can also rename the file once the command is given. Moreover, OS returns group id and process user id when it receives a command.

Another platform for Python programming is iso, a packaging used to simplify the development cycle linked to building-machine learning models. It also comes in handy during deployment. Iso is commonly used because it is effective and reliable. It promotes mental clarity when designing learning algorithms. Some platforms are hectic to use and can make one give up on the creation process. Instead of helping you come up with something that is unique, it makes you frustrated. The worst thing that can happen during the development of machine

66

learning models is for the creator to become frustrated. It makes the entire process cumbersome and does not yield good results. Instead of using a platform that you unsure of, it is better to use one that guarantees results. There are few platforms that guarantee results, and one should take advantage of them. iso is also effective because it allows developers to understand the problem they are dealing with. It makes everything clear and allows the user to e fulfilled from creating the models. Iso is special because it can define modular data changes that form part of the model, which helps developers to stay organized. It also makes the transition from one model to another easy. Another advantage of iso is that it has tools that can be used for data augmentation. One can also save and deploy models easily. It also enables interactions with the model building process, unlike other platforms. Iso is good because it has tools which enable users to transform responses and predictors in one step. It saves time and allows you to learn a lot from the process. It yields more results when used with other python programming tools/platforms. Moreover, it is flexible and allows users to concentrate on other things while using it. It is not restrictive, and users and free in the platform.

Chapter 8: Decision Trees

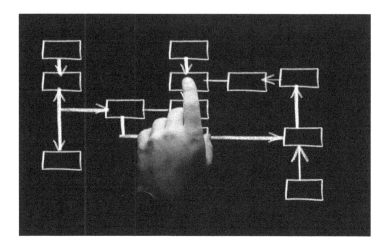

A decision tree is a decision-support tool with a tree that utilizes tree-like graphs to explain concepts. It uses utility, resources costs, and event outcomes. It is suitable for showing algorithms with only conditional control statements. In a decision tree, every internal note symbolizes a test on the attribute while the branch stands for the results of the test. Leaf nodes represent class labels and the distance from the root to the leaf signify the classification rules. Decision trees are helpful in learning algorithms and are widely used. Moreover, tree-based learning algorithms are popular learning methods. Some of the reasons why decision trees are common are because they empower predictive models with straightforward interpretation and efficiency. They are also accurate, stable, and reliable. They are also ideal for linear mapping models, unlike other tools. Decision trees solve all kind of challenges and never disappoint. Many people attest to the fact that this decision-support tool has helped them overcome problems and reach the helm. Decision tree algorithms are known as Classification and Regression Trees (CART). It is useful for tackling data science challenges. In a decision tree, the term Root Node stands for the entire population, which is divided further into homogenous groups. When sub-nodes are split further, they are referred to as decision nodes. Splitting is the act of dividing nodes into sub-nodes.

Pruning refers to the process of removing sub-nodes of decision nodes. Decision trees are made in such a way that they fit easily in programmatic structures. They are laid out to categorize issues when they arise. People can use decision trees to know the species of plants. There are many assumptions people make when creating decision trees. Many people consider the entire training set as a root in the beginning. Records are divided based on attribute values. Most people prefer feature values to be categorical. Below is an example of a decision tree.

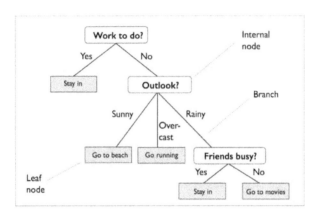

Decision trees are used for several reasons. Data miners use decision trees to analyze data. It is also commonly used in machine learning and similar activities. For example, decision trees can be used to evaluate opportunities for brand expansion using historical sales data. It can also be used to determine possible customers using demographic data. Many companies use decision trees to evaluate their performance in the market and determine their buyers. This allows them to adjust their marketing tactics to suit the target customers. It also informs them of problematic areas and how to approach buyers. Knowing possible buyers enables a firm to limit its advertising budget. Most of the time, companies spend a lot of money creating adverts without knowing where to target. They end up with more losses than profits. They are not able to recover even when a product makes massive sales. Decision trees are also used to predict the possibility of a default borrower using the predictive model. One of the reasons why companies go bankrupt is because of default borrowers. Some people do not keep their word when it comes to returning borrowed money. To evade such individuals, companies can use predictive models obtained from historical data to know such people. Doing this saves both time and operations of the company. Decision trees are also used in operations research to know a strategy that has a high chance of meeting set targets. There is no need in doing a research without knowing its end goal. A decision tree helps in performing decision analysis and makes work easy for researchers. Many industries have used decision trees to interpret data, including engineering, financial, energy, education, and business. People who were using other tools and techniques to analyze data have switched to decision tree because of its benefits.

Decision trees have numerous advantages that make them worthwhile. They are easy to understand. There are several tools that are used to solve problems, but most of them are hectic and need skills. On the contrary, decision trees are simple and do not require a lot of attention to understand. Even people without analytical knowledge can use a decision tree. It is not a must to have statistical knowledge to understand decision tree algorithms. The graphical representations used are simple, and users can relate to the narrative. Moreover, they have a simple hypothesis that users can relate to. Decision trees are effective in data exploration. They are useful in identifying the best variable and links between variables. For the longest time, people used variables that did not yield results. Researchers were frustrated because they could not explore data fully, decision trees changed the narrative. Now researchers can explore data with ease. Moreover, they can create new variables to predict target variables. If we are dealing with an issue where we have data on thousands of variables, decision trees save you from the struggle of finding the most significant one. Another added advantage of the decision tree is that users only put in little effort to prepare data. Less data cleaning for users allows them to focus on other things. It is effective and reliable, compared to other modeling techniques. Furthermore, decision tree is not influenced by missing values or outliers. It is also a non-parametric method which means that they have no assumptions about the classifier structure and space distributions.

Despite its benefits, decision tree has disadvantages that users should keep in mind. In some cases, decision-tree learners might create trees that do not generate expected results. In such cases, the user is left wondering whether it was a good idea to use a decision tree. It can be frustrating if misused. The case of creating a complex tree is known as over fitting, and many people fall under this category. Learners solve this problem by setting constraints on model parameters. They can also prune it to deal with the issue. Another challenge with decision tree is the fact that it does not fit continuous variables. If you are working with a continuous numerical variable, you stand a high chance of losing information. Moreover, decision tends to be unstable in case the tree is altered. One is supposed to use the tree as it is because a slight variable can result in a completely different thing. There are greedy algorithms which do not guarantee a return to the decision tree. Learners can eliminate this problem by training several trees. They also have to be careful when creating a decision tree. Decision trees do an excellent job in determining variables, but require careful mitigation to avoid errors. There is no guarantee of a good outcome and the user must constantly monitor it to interpret its performance.

At the bottom of the decision tree lies the terminal nodes. Terminal nodes are bottom because decision trees are drawn upside down. Classification trees and regression trees have similarities and differences. Both work in a similar way only that regression trees in instances where dependent variables are continuous. On the contrary, classification trees are employed whenever dependent variables are categorical. Both trees are known to divide the predictor space into separate regions. They also take a greedy approach and continue until the criteria stipulated by the user are met. Moreover, the splitting process contributes to full developed trees until the set criteria are reached. However, there is a possibility that the grown tree might overfit data, and this is where pruning comes in. Deciding to split a tree affects its performance. It can derail or improve accuracy, based on it is done. The decision criteria vary depending on whether it is for regression trees or classification trees. Several algorithms are used when deciding whether to split a decision tree into sub-nodes. The target variable affects the purity of the node. After splitting the node on present variables, decision trees pick the one with more homogenous sub-nodes.

A tree has several uses in real life, and it turns out that it is also applicable in machine learning. It can be used to represent decisions virtually in decision analysis. The question that running people's minds is how an algorithm can be represented by a tree. Similar to how a real-life tree has many parts, decision trees also have several parts which perform different functions. It is essential to understand all the parts in a decision tree and their role. While the dataset has more features, we cannot overlook the simplicity of a decision tree. For someone to grow a tree, he/she must decide the features to use and conditions that are favorable for splitting. The person also needs to know when to stop. Trimming the tree is important because it grows habitually. You also need to be patient when creating a decision tree. Similar to how a real-life tree takes time to grow and goes through the pruning process, you must be patient when creating a decision tree. Rushing the process may cause overfitting so it is better to take time and do a good job. There are various techniques used for splitting, including recursive binary splitting, where all the features of taken into account a cost function is used to test split points. Many people do not know when to stop splitting a tree. Overdoing it can cause more problems than expected, and it is important to stop at the right time. Huge trees lead to overfitting, and one way of avoiding this is setting a minimum number of training input for every leaf. Some people are skeptical about this strategy, but it works for many. Users need to find methods that work and stick to them. What works for one may not do the same for another user.

Decision trees use algorithms such as Gini Index, and Chi-Square to determine the most homogenous nodes. Gini Index states that if one picks two items from a sample randomly, they must be in the same class and the probability of this happening is 1. The value of homogeneity increases with a high value of Gini. CART utilizes Gini Index technique to create binary splits. Chi-Square is another algorithm used by decision trees to calculate variables. It is used to determine statistical significance between the parent node and sub-nodes. It is measured by the value of squares of standard differences between expected and observed frequencies. You can derive Chi-Square for each node by calculating the deviation for both success and failure. The good news is that impure nodes need less information to describe and vice versa. Some steps can be taken to avoid over-fitting to improve efficiency of decision trees. Over-fitting is one of the problems faced by decision trees. Dealing with it means that users will have wonderful experiences using the decision-making support tool. A model with over-fitting issue when it attempts to reduce training set mistakes, but causes more test set errors. You can deal with the issue of overfitting by pruning and putting limits on the tree size. You can set limits on the tree size by employing numerous parameters that define a tree. The parameters include minimum populations for a node split, minimum sample for the leaf, maximum vertical depth, increased features to weigh for a split, and increased terminal node. Regarding minimum population for the node split, indicate the minimum number of samples needed in a node to qualify for splitting. This sample can be used to control over-fitting. Use higher values to prevent models from learning relations which is significant in the decision tree. Use minimum samples for the terminal leaf. Start by defining the samples needed in a terminal leaf. It is also used to control over-fitting like the minimum samples for node split. Use lower values for class problems that are imbalanced.

Alternatively, use the tree pruning method to deal with the issue of over-fitting. The method of putting limitations is a greedy tactic which looks for the best split available and moves on until the specified point is reached. The difference between putting limitations and pruning is that the former cannot see the danger ahead and adopt a greedy approach to overcome it. The pruning method allows you to see what is ahead and helps you to make the right choice. To implement pruning in a decision tree, we start by creating the tree then start removing leaves at the bottom. Remove the leaves that do not yield good returns when compared with the top. It is important to note that not every problem can be addressed using linear methods. There are amazing non-linear methods that perform wonders and users need to try them. Tree-based models can map non-linearity better than most techniques. Decision trees are ideal because they can also be used to solve classification and regression challenges.

There are two types of decision trees and they are based on target variables available. The first type of a decision tree is Categorical Variable Decision Tree. This is a decision tree with categorical target variables. In the example of which students will play baseball, where the target variable was learners will play baseball or not, that is yes or no. The second type is the Continuous Variable Decision Tree. As the name suggests, this type of decision tree contains continuous target variables. For instance, if there is a problem to predict whether clients will pay their renewal premiums (yes/no), it is apparent that income is a notable variable in them paying premiums, but insurance firms may lack income information about clients. To solve this problem, we can create a decision tree to predict the income of all clients. The insurance company will take into consideration the occupation when creating the decision tree. Values for continuous variable are being predicted in this case. The first thing is to put the best attribute at the root of the tree. Afterward, split the training set and make sure that each subset has data. Start from the root of the tree when predicting a class label for records. Values of the root attribute will be compared with record's attributes. The most important thing during this process is to use the right data to minimize errors. By comparing attribute values with internal nodes, we increase chances of getting the right variable. Decision trees work in a simple way. It falls in the category of supervised learning algorithm with a predefined target variable used to classify challenges. Both continuous input and categorical output variables use decision trees. It divides the population into two homogenous sets, depending on the differentiator. For example, if we have a sample of 20 learners with variables gender (girl/boy), height (4 to 5 ft) and class (IV/V). 10 out of the learners play baseball and we want to create a model to predict who is likely to play baseball. To do so, we have to separate learners who play baseball depending on highly significant input variable and this is where one uses a decision tree. The decision tree separate learners based on the values of the three variables and determine which one makes the best homogenous sets. By identifying the best variable among the three, it helps in solving the problem. It utilizes numerous algorithms to identify the significant variable.

Creating Our Own Decision Tree

Now that we have had a bit of time to talk about the decision trees and how they are supposed to work, it is time to create one of our own. These are actually a lot easier and simpler to work with compared to what it sounds like, but it is going to be so useful to work with. So, let's spend some time taking a look at the steps that we are able to use in order to create one of our own decision trees and make this process work well for us.

Decision trees are going to be one of the most popular algorithms that we can work with, mostly because it is so powerful to use. The algorithm that comes with the decision tree is going to be one of our supervised learning algorithms, and it is going to work with both the categorical and the continuous variables that you use for your output.

In the code that we are going to work with in a bit, there are a number of different packages that we need to import and work with in order to make this work. We will focus on the Pandas, the NumPy, and the sklearn packages to get them to work the best way possible. If you do not have these on your computer already, then now is the time to get them on so that you can use them for your needs.

While we are here, we need to make a few assumptions for the decision tree to work. If these are not true, then the results of our decision tree may not work the way that we want. Some of the assumptions that we have to make with this one will include:

1. When we first start with this, we need to consider all of our set of training data as the root of the tree. We can change that later if needed.
2. Attributes are going to be assumed as categorical for all of the information gain. And when we are working with the gini index, we are going to assume that the attributes are continuous in nature.
3. When we look just on the basis of the attribute values, this

means that the records are going to be distributed in a recursive manner.

4. We are also able to work with some of the statistical methods to help order the attributes either as the internal node or as part of the root.

There is also a bit of pseudocode that we need to work with along the way. To do this, we need to work with a number of steps along the way. Some of these steps will include:

1. Find the attribute that looks the best out of all of them and then place it right on the root node of your tree.
2. When this is done, you can split the training set of the dataset into subsets. While you are making one of these subsets you have to make sure that all of the subsets of training the dataset should come in with the same value for that attribute.
3. You are able to find the leaf nodes to all of your branches when you go through and repeat one and two on all of your subsets.

While we are implementing our decision tree, we are going to end up with two phases that we need to focus on. These include the building phase and the operational phase. In our building phase, we are going to do a number of things that include preprocessing our data set, splitting up the set of data that we are working with so that we end up with the training and the testing set to work on the algorithm. Then we are able to train the classifier. And then we can move on to the operational phase. This is the part where we are able to use the algorithm in order to make some predictions, and it is a good way to calculate how accurate things are for us along the way. The next step that we need to work with here is doing a data import. This can be done with the help of our pandas package that we can get with Python. Here, we are going to be able to work with a URL that is going to be directly able to fetch the dataset from the UCI site, and we will not have to take the time to download the set of data. When you try to get this code to execute on the system, it is important to make sure that the internet connection is on and working well. As the set of data is going to be separated out by the ",", so we have to make sure that we pass the sep parameters value as ",". Another thing that we are going to notice when we are working with this one is that the set of data that we are working with is not going to contain the header, so we need to go through and pass the parameter value of our header as none. If we do not pass this parameter for the header, ten it will consider the first line of the set of data for the header.

Then it is time to go through and do some data slicing. Before we train our data and start to use it with the algorithm, we need to make sure that we can split the set of data into both of the options for the training and the testing. In order to go through our set of data and split it up into training and testing, we need to bring out a module from sklearn that is noted as train_test_split. To go through this, we are going to separate out the target variable from the attributes that are found in our set of data. Then we are able to go through and split up the data for the purposes of training and testing. Take your time doing this because it is going to make a big difference in how well the algorithm is going to be prepared to do some of the work that we want it too.

There are a few other things that we need to go through and understand a bit more as we work with this process. First, we have the idea of entropy here. This is going to be an important thing to measure because it will tell us the uncertainty of our random variable, and it is going to be able to help us to characterize the impurity of our arbitrary collection of examples. In our decision tree, the higher we see the entropy, the more the information content that is there. The entropy typically changes when we work with a node in the decision tree to help us create a new partition for the training instances, making them into smaller subsets. We have to do a few different iterations of the training and then testing, going back and forth, so we need to divide these up so we can accomplish that a few more times. Then there is the information gain, which is going to help us o know a bit more about measuring the change in entropy. Sklearn is going to be useful here because it is able to support the criteria of entropy for our information gain. We do need to make sure that we go through and use the method of information gain, and we have to actually mention that we want this explicitly. Along with this, we are going to be able to work with the accuracy score, which is going to be there to help us figure out how accurate the trained classifier is. And finally, we can use the confusion matrix in our code to help us to understand the behavior of the trained classifier over the test set of data or to validate the set of data that we are working with.

Now that we have had some time to go through the different parts that are necessary when we work with our decision trees, it is time for us to take this to the next part and look at some of the coding that we are able to work with. Some of the coding that a programmer is able to use to create our own decision trees, and use all of the steps that we had above, will include:

```
# Importing the required packages

import numpy as np

import pandas as pd

from sklearn.metrics import confusion_matrix

from sklearn.cross_validation import train_test_split

from sklearn.tree import DecisionTreeClassifier

from sklearn.metrics import accuracy_score

from sklearn.metrics import classification_report


# Function importing Dataset
def importdata():

    balance_data = pd.read_csv(
```

```python
    'https://archive.ics.uci.edu/ml/machine-learning-'+
    'databases/balance-scale/balance-scale.data',
        sep= ',', header = None)


        # Printing the dataswet shape
        print ("Dataset Length: ", len(balance_data))
        print ("Dataset Shape: ", balance_data.shape)


        # Printing the dataset obseravtions
        print ("Dataset: ",balance_data.head())
        return balance_data


# Function to split the dataset
def splitdataset(balance_data):
    # Separating the target variable
    X = balance_data.values[:, 1:5]
    Y = balance_data.values[:, 0]


    # Splitting the dataset into train and test
    X_train, X_test, y_train, y_test = train_test_split(
```

```
        X, Y, test_size = 0.3, random_state = 100)


    return X, Y, X_train, X_test, y_train, y_test


# Function to perform training with giniIndex.
def train_using_gini(X_train, X_test, y_train):


    # Creating the classifier object
    clf_gini = DecisionTreeClassifier(criterion = "gini",
            random_state = 100,max_depth=3, min_samples_leaf=5)


    # Performing training
    clf_gini.fit(X_train, y_train)
    return clf_gini
# Function to perform training with entropy.
def tarin_using_entropy(X_train, X_test, y_train):


    # Decision tree with entropy
    clf_entropy = DecisionTreeClassifier(
            criterion = "entropy", random_state = 100,
```

```python
                max_depth = 3, min_samples_leaf = 5)


    # Performing training

    clf_entropy.fit(X_train, y_train)

    return clf_entropy


# Function to make predictions

def prediction(X_test, clf_object):


    # Predicton on test with giniIndex

    y_pred = clf_object.predict(X_test)

    print("Predicted values:")

    print(y_pred)

    return y_pred

# Function to calculate accuracy

def cal_accuracy(y_test, y_pred):


    print("Confusion Matrix: ",

        confusion_matrix(y_test, y_pred))
```

```python
    print ("Accuracy : ",
    accuracy_score(y_test,y_pred)*100)

    print("Report : ",
    classification_report(y_test, y_pred))

# Driver code
def main():

    # Building Phase
    data = importdata()
    X, Y, X_train, X_test, y_train, y_test = splitdataset(data)
    clf_gini = train_using_gini(X_train, X_test, y_train)
    clf_entropy = tarin_using_entropy(X_train, X_test, y_train)

    # Operational Phase
    print("Results Using Gini Index:")

    # Prediction using gini
    y_pred_gini = prediction(X_test, clf_gini)
```

```python
    cal_accuracy(y_test, y_pred_gini)


    print("Results Using Entropy:")

    # Prediction using entropy

    y_pred_entropy = prediction(X_test, clf_entropy)

    cal_accuracy(y_test, y_pred_entropy)


# Calling main function

if __name__=="__main__":

    main()
```

Chapter 9 : K-Nearest Neighbors (KNN)

The K-Nearest Neighbors is the simplest and the most used learning algorithms in classification and regression problems. This type is straightforward and easy to master. The value of a result for the solved puzzle is based on the selection made by the neighboring values. The purpose of this is to classify the most common class, following its K-nearest neighbors. KNN is sometimes used in a regression where the value of output is predicted as per the most continuous value. The output value can be a mean or median of the entire class (k-nearest neighbors). In both regression and classification problems, the value input that corresponds to k and is used for training is usually found in the feature space. The desired result depends on the type of machine learning for which KNN has been used, that is to say, either classification r regression.

In simple terms, the KNN algorithm can be defined as one that classifies objects by putting them to the group they are close to. The method takes into account the features and data points in a set. Fr the algorithmic function, the process will try to find out a group in which object X belongs to by looking at the ends near object X in the same state. A result is founded by determining where the majority features

84

lie. For example, if most of the points of an object fall in group Y, then object X is classified in group Y. This method of identifying a group in which item X belongs is used in classification. It works in the same way as a plural vote for the neighbors, and then the item is allocated a group in which the majority of its k nearest neighbors fall in. When the evaluation is done, and the value of k comes out as 1, then the object is classified in that same class.

KNN is sometimes referred to the lazy learner because it takes time to compute values. KNN is based on estimations, and the mathematical analysis is usually left pending up to the last step of classification.

In both regression and classification problems, a single unit should be set as the average of a class. This is to ensure that the closest neighbor in that unit contributes to the metric more than the neighbors that lie far from the class. For instance, a good model will set a value at $1/x$, where the x is the distance between the nearest neighbors.

For classification problems, the neighbors are chosen from units with a known value in terms of features and other parameters. The group can be considered as training datasets even though less training is done in the K nearest neighbor theory. A distinctive characteristic of the k nearest algorithm is its sensitivity to the components and the composition of a dataset. An example of training data that can be used for k nearest neighbor algorithm is a labeled vector, usually applied in feature space that has many dimensions. The algorithms learn by isolating feature vectors and the labeled classes in the training dataset. In the process of classifying objects, the value of k is usually constant and set by the user of the system. In the process, a vector without a label (used a testing data) is assigned a group by looking at the labels that frequently appear throughout the training set and is the closest to the vector. The training data set is also called the k sample.

For a continuous variable, the Euclidean distance is the commonly used parameter for solving range related problems. For variables that are not continuous, also referred to as separate, a different setting is used to solve the problem. The performance of the nearest algorithm can be enhanced by the incorporation of other unique algorithms to study the elements that define the distance space.

Finding the Value of K in the K Nearest Algorithm

In the opening segment of this chapter, I mentioned that the k value is a constant that is set by the user of the system. That statement remains the case. However, it takes a lot to choose the value that best represents k. I this sector I want to raw a theory that can help in settling for the real value of k. the first thing to note is that the selection of k factor is dependent on the type and weight of data. Another metric that influences the choice of k is the type of function, that is, whether the task is classification or regression. The features of the object also play a more significant role in choosing the k value. Lastly, the choice of k is primarily put on the shoulders of the user (that is why the algorithms are mostly prone to bias). From all this we can conclude that the k factor has a close relationship with the system in which it is used. The most applicable implication is the weight of data.

When the set value of k is significant, there are chances that noise will be reduced within the datasets. However, an important k factor results in undifferentiated boundaries within classes. Therefore, the best value of k can only be arrived by a trial and error method that is based mostly on experiments. The experiments are. In other words, called optimization processes. These processes are aimed at correcting deviations of metric values form the low point, leading to a point where a unit can be predicted to be the closest to the k sample. At this point, the value of k should be 1. This is the process referred to as the nearest neighbor algorithm.

Noise, bias, or any other undesirable parameter can significantly alter the accuracy of the K- nearest neighbor algorithm. Efficacy is also complicated by the inconsistency of features to the roles of the system. For example, a system that is supposed to predict whether part of the population is men or women may not be accurate in predicting other metrics. Such parameters may be whether the same section of the community is rich or poor. This problem, however, can be solved by isolating features to reflect the functions of the algorithm and the desired result. The isolation can be done by the use of an evolutionary algorithm or by mutually incorporating the k sample (training dataset) with the data to be classified.

In a joint classification problem, also called binary, the k value is recommended to be an odd number. In that way, we avoid the problem of seeing a tie between elements. If the k value proves challenging to estimate, it is recommended that you use a bootstrap method to evaluate it.

Comparing the K Nearest Neighbor with the K Means Clustering

I cannot summarize this chapter without comparing the most commonly used algorithms in machine learning. The two algorithms (k- means clustering and k nearest neigh our), are usually mistaken for each other because of the k letter in their names. The clearest distinction between the two algorithms is that k-means is an unsupervised algorithm while the k-nearest neighbor is a supervised algorithm. The functions also can be used to differentiate the two complex algorithms. The c means is used for clustering while the k nearest algorithm is used for classification and sometimes in regression problems.

The K-Nearest Neighbors Algorithm

The first thing to note is that this is a supervised algorithm it is used for both classification and regression problems. Being a supervised algorithm, the k nearest uses learning data that are labeled. The KNN learns from the data and is thus able to classify unlabeled data by looking at the value of k in the nearest data points within the class. The k value in the algorithm is set by the developer of the system, as mentioned above.

The K-Means Algorithm

Compared to the KNN algorithm, the K-means algorithm is an unsupervised type that is used for clustering problems. Being an unsupervised algorithm, the k-means do not rely on labeled data to make predictions.

The k means algorithm can cluster objects by studying the distance between the data points in a class over time. Here, the value of k is said to reflect the number of classes that are supposed to be analyzed — the k-means works by minimizing error.

Differences Between the KNN and the KM

K-means algorithm is used in situations where the attributes of the data are not known, such as estimating the fall and rise of stock value over time. On the other hand, the K-nearest neighbor algorithm is used for classification and regression purposes, where the metrics are clearly stated. The function of the k-means can broaden to cover the results of the k-nearest neighbor algorithm. This is to say that, when the k-nearest algorithm predicts an event, the k-means can be used to analyze the result further. Analyzation may be in ways that give a more in-depth understanding of the features and the outcome.

For this reason, both algorithms are vital in components of machine learning. Nonetheless, the two algorithms are used in different circumstances to solve various problems, while deriving the function k and what it represents in the system. Using the k factor, this statement can be shortened as;

    i.   K-means, being an unsupervised algorithm, works by collecting data in groups to form a k number of clusters.

    ii.   K nearest neighbor, being a supervised algorithm, works by producing new data using the metrics in the learning data. KNN does this to assign points according to the k value, which represents the nearest point of data.

Despite the difference in scope and functions, both the k nearest neighbor algorithm and the k means algorithm work by considering distance within the dataset.

Limitation of the K Nearest Neighbor Algorithm

A significant limitation of the classification method of k nearest neighbor is the existence of bias among the classes. If the distribution of elements in the class is twisted, the majority of items within the unit will tilt the metrics to their side. For instance, the dominant feature within the feature space will attract the estimating to their points because they are found almost everywhere within the unit. However, such bias can be alleviated in many ways. The most common method of overcoming prejudice is by setting an average metric point in the class. The balance is found when the distance between the k nearest neighbor is considerably weighted.

Solving the problem of bias in regression requires a different approach. A unit of the k nearest neighbors is crossed by an average weight value that is inversely proportional to the distance between the two points in the group. This is the distance from the nearest neighbor to the test point. An additional method to be used can be the generalization of the data representing each class. A case in point is representative nodes in the self-organizing map, which represent the core point of the dataset. The central location is, Therefore, regardless of the distribution of elements in the class.

Advantages of K Nearest Neighbors

Being the easiest and the simplest of all machine learning algorithms, the k nearest neighbor's algorithm boasts of many positives.

The k nearest neighbor is also referred to as the lazy learner. This name comes from the fact that the algorithm does not learn anything during the training period. However, it gains on occasions where it is required to perform a task. The lack of training period can be seen as a win on its side. The algorithm stores sets of learning data and uses it when it is required to make predictions. The process ensures that the KNN algorithm is the fastest among the machine learning algorithms, which need training.

Additional sets of data can be induced in the k-nearest neighbor flawlessly without altering the prediction accuracy. This is supported by the fact that it does not require training.

The k nearest neighbor algorithm only requires two metrics to function. The two parameters are the k factor and the distance function. This makes the algorithm simple and easy to device.

Disadvantages of K nearest neighbor

The algorithm cannot be effective when handling large amounts of data. Large sets of data present a wide range between points, which make the algorithm ineffective.

As seen in the paragraph above, the algorithm cannot work with large dimensions. When the distribution of data is broad, the estimation of the distance between the nearest points becomes a challenge.

K nearest neighbor algorithm is susceptible to noise and other irregularities in data. For effectiveness, manual methods are incorporated to remove outliers and induce values that are not in the system.

The algorithm usually requires regular feature scaling.

Creating Our Own KNN Algorithm

Now it is time for us to go through and create one of our own KNN algorithms and use this for our own needs in our data analysis. The KNN algorithm that we have been talking about so far is going to use the feature similarity, which is going to help predict the values of the new points of data, which further means that all of the new points of data are going to be assigned a value based on how well they are able to match the points that are found in our training set. We are able to better understand this with some of the following steps along the way.

1. First, we need to make sure that we start with implementing our algorithm. And this is going to require us to have a set of data to work with. So, while we are working with the first step of this algorithm, we need to load the training and the testing data that we want to use.
2. Next, we have to go through and choose what the value of K should be. This can be any integer that we want, but will help us to separate out the data we are working with.
3. For all of the points that are going to be in our test data, there are a few things that we need to accomplish, and these steps will include:
    a. We have to start with this one to calculate the distance between the data for the testing, and then each row of

the training data with the help of any methods that you want to use. These include options like Hamming or Manhattan distance, and the Euclidean distance. The most common of these is going to be the Euclidean distance.

  b. Now, based on the value that you place with the distance, we want to go through and sort this out in ascending order.

  c. When that order is all done, it is time for us to go through and choose out the top K rows based on the sorted arrays that we are working with.

  d. And then, we can end this part by assigning a class to our point for testing. The class that we are going to assign here is going to be based on the class that is the most frequent for these rows.

4. When we are done with all of this, then the algorithm is going to end, and we should be able to take a look at the clustering and how it is going to work for us.

This is going to take a bit of work to accomplish, but you will find that it is going to help us get a lot of things done in the process. And when it shows up, the graph or the chart will show us where our data points are supposed to go, and that will help us to take a look at where these points go, and learn some of the new options that we could explore to make this work for us.

Chapter 10: Random Forest Algorithms with Python

This type of algorithm is the most available and common in recent years. There are several factors that you need to comprehend this type of algorithm. The main objective of this algorithm is to help with the regression and classification computations using the raw natural data. When you talk of a random forest, you refer to a collection of learning methods with multiple decision trees. Random forest improves in outcome prediction by calculating the average of the decision trees impacts. With this, you can make several predictions using the various models provided in this algorithm. Examples of models you can correctly use include the logistic regression, which mainly deals with binomial data. The other examples might include k-nearest neighbours, naïve Bayes and even support vector machines. In most cases, it works best where different features of a model comprise of predictive power which is very weak but shows stronger power in a combination. The following illustrations will help you understand this topic very well.

The Decision Trees

They refer to predictive models for calculating some target values using binary rules. It comprises of two forms or types, for example, regression trees and classification. Regression trees are applicable in creating any continuous data like those data sets used in tree cover percentage and also in biomass. On the other hand, classification trees deal with sets of data which are very definite and specific. Examples are data found within the land cover. It is good to note that any typical tree composed of leaves, nodes and even branches. As a result of all these features, it will lead to a simple model. In this case, the nodes comprise of some unique attributes that are entirely applicable in the functioning of your algorithm. You also need to take a look at the random forest so that you increase your level of understanding about this topic.

The Random Forest

From the layman's language, you can deduce that random forests consist of a collection of tree predictors in that every individual tree will strictly depend on random vector values which have been independently sampled and distributed equally to all different trees within the forest. You can also say that random forest can be a form of a classifier comprising of a group of trees which have been arranged structurally as classifiers. Therefore, in brief, you can conclude that random forest has the abilities to build up various multiple trees decisions and later on fuse them to come up with the stable prediction and which is highly accurate. It is also good to note that this kind of machine learning algorithm entirely relies on ensemble learning. Therefore, ensemble learning is a form of learning where you can categorically join all algorithms of different types or same types so as to come up with a model which is very powerful in terms of predictions. Funny enough, random forests come as a result of the combination of multiple different trees used in decision making. Therefore, you can also refer to it as 'forest of trees.'

Merits of Random Forest

- It is certainly applicable to both regression problems and classification.

- It helps in reducing overfitting, especially within the trees. All these are possible through performing averaging.

- It is the most accurate algorithm since it will only give a wrong prediction if, at all, more than half of the data used are wrong.

- It is easy to use since you can easily detect the level of importance or instead of the significance of every feature, especially within the prediction. In this case, Sklearn boasts of its powerful library in performing that task.

- The algorithm reduces the traces of biasedness within the analysis since it mainly depends on the entire crowd of the forest for its maximum prediction.

- It is a highly stable algorithm which you can trust with all your computations. A slight mistake will only affect a small portion of the prediction. Therefore, the whole prediction will still be correct.

- This type of algorithm can perform its duties using numerical and categorical features.

Demerits of Random Forests

- It has an annoying and overlapping trend of overfitting on some sets of data, especially the ones with regression tasks and also the noisy classification.

- It's a costly and highly complex algorithm as compared to other algorithms such as decision tree algorithm.

- Its training takes long since it comprises a large combination of decision trees.

Decision tree and random forests algorithms have different roles in data computations and outcome predictions. Again, the two have a specific time of implementation. That's, the exact time you can eventually apply them in real life. Below illustrations give us enough explanations on when to use these two aspects of data prediction algorithms.

When do we apply the decision tree:
- You can use the decision tree when you prefer the simplicity of your model with many explainable attributes.
- You can also use this method, especially when you want your model to be non-parametric.
- You can also apply this when you are not worrying any form of multicollinearity or something to do with regularization or feature selection.

When do we apply random forest:
- When you require good data prediction accuracy even though you don't worry about model interpretations.
- When you are looking for accuracy while using a validation data set.

How to Perform the Random Forest Algorithm
The illustrations below show a clear step by step guideline on how to accomplish this kind of algorithm.

1. You can start by picking a random number like say X from the random records within the sets of data.
2. Try as much as possible to come up with a decision tree, basing your computations on X records.
3. You can now choose the number you require especially the number of trees. Then, you can repeat these steps that's step 1 and 2.
4. For example, if you are solving a regression problem, dealing with a new record, every individual tree in those particular

forests will have an output value of Y. In this case, you can quickly get the final value by computing the average of all the predictions.

5. Also, if it is a classification problem, the predictions narrow to an individual tree that's, every tree takes part in categorical predictions which comprise of new recordings. Eventually, the category with the majority votes will have the power to handle the new records.

Feature Selection Methods in Random Forest

Random forests boast of being popular within the technological world. The main attributes towards this are their robustness, accuracy and also you can use them more easily. It provides two strict methods that you can employ in your feature selection, as shown in the illustrations below.

The Mean Decrease Impurity

Random forests comprise of various decision trees. Each node in that decision trees represents a situation of only one single feature. The primary function of this node here is to split those datasets into two equal parts in that same set will have similar values at the end. All these happen at the optimal level condition which you can refer to as impurity. However, in classification, you can call it Gini impurity or instead information gain, which is also entropy.

In most cases, you can call it variance in regression. Therefore, when having some sorts of tree training, you can eventually compute the amount reduced by each feature on the impurity, which is weighted. In the case of a forest, you can calculate the decreased impurity by getting their average and later on ranking them using the same measure.

However, in this method, there are things of great importance to keep in your mind. The first one is that when you compute more categories, the chances of getting biased is high. The next thing to keep in mind is that it treats all the correlated features equally, but when you take one as a predictor, then the importance of the rest reduces. This is because one feature reduces the impurities of the other features.

The Mean Decrease Accuracy

This category involves getting the accuracy of impacts features by measuring them directly. The main objective here is to detect the level of reduction inaccuracy caused by the permutation, especially within the accuracy model.

Creating Our Own Random Forests

Now that we have had a chance to go through and learn about the random forest, it is time for us to go through and actually perform one of these algorithms for our own. There are a few options and steps that we want to be able to work with in order to get the Random Forest to behave in the manner that we would like. Some of the steps that we are able to use n order to work with the random forest algorithm include:

1. Pick out the N random records that are a part of our set of data.
2. Then we are able to take those records and then build up the decision tree to start with. Remember that we need to have several of these decision trees in order to end up with a random forest, so starting with one is important.
3. We can then go through and choose how many trees we would like to have with our algorithm before going through and repeating the first two steps again with each one.
4. If we are doing this to work with one of the regression problems for a new record that we want to use, each tree in the forest is going to be able to predict the value of Y, which is going to be our output. The final value is then going to be calculated by taking the average of the values predicted by all of the trees that you have in your forest.

a. Or, if you are going to use this to work with a classification problem, each tree that is in the forest needs to be able to predict the category that our new records are able to belong to. Finally, the new record is going to be assigned to the category that is able to win the vote of the majority.

#' reg_rf

#' Fits a random forest with a continuous scaled features and target

#' variable (regression)

#'

#' @param formula an object of class formula

#' @param n_trees an integer specifying the number of trees to sprout

#' @param feature_frac an numeric value defined between [0,1]

#'   specifies the percentage of total features to be used in

#'   each regression tree

#' @param data a data.frame or matrix

#'

#' @importFrom plyr raply

#' @return

#' @export

#'

```r
#' @examples # Complete runthrough see:
www.github.com/andrebleier/cheapml

reg_rf <- function(formula, n_trees, feature_frac, data) {



  # source the regression tree function

  source("algorithms/reg_tree_imp.R")



  # load plyr

  require(plyr)



  # define function to sprout a single tree

  sprout_tree <- function(formula, feature_frac, data) {
    # extract features

    features <- all.vars(formula)[-1]



    # extract target

    target <- all.vars(formula)[1]



    # bag the data

    # - randomly sample the data with replacement (duplicate are
possible)
```

```r
train <-
  data[sample(1:nrow(data), size = nrow(data), replace = TRUE)]


  # randomly sample features
  # - only fit the regression tree with feature_frac * 100 % of the
features
  features_sample <- sample(features,
                  size = ceiling(length(features) * feature_frac),
                  replace = FALSE)


  # create new formula
  formula_new <-
    as.formula(paste0(target, " ~ ", paste0(features_sample,
                      collapse = " + ")))


  # fit the regression tree
  tree <- reg_tree_imp(formula = formula_new,
              data = train,
              minsize = ceiling(nrow(train) * 0.1))


  # save the fit and the importance
```

```
  return(list(tree$fit, tree$importance))

}


# apply the rf_tree function n_trees times with plyr::raply
# - track the progress with a progress bar
trees <- plyr::raply(

  n_trees,

  sprout_tree(

    formula = formula,

    feature_frac = feature_frac,

    data = data

  ),

  .progress = "text"

)


# extract fit
fits <- do.call("cbind", trees[, 1])


# calculate the final fit as a mean of all regression trees
rf_fit <- apply(fits, MARGIN = 1, mean)
```

```
# extract the feature importance

imp_full <- do.call("rbind", trees[, 2])



# build the mean feature importance between all trees

imp <- aggregate(IMPORTANCE ~ FEATURES, FUN = mean,
imp_full)



# build the ratio for interpretation purposes

imp$IMPORTANCE <- imp$IMPORTANCE /
sum(imp$IMPORTANCE)



# export

return(list(fit = rf_fit,

        importance = imp[order(imp$IMPORTANCE, decreasing =
TRUE), ]))

}
```

In Summary

Random forests form a large part in the methods used to solve day to day problems and tasks using a computer. They are high in terms of feature ranking since you can easily apply them. It is also good to note that Random Forest minimal engineering techniques towards its feature. Also, it doesn't need much care of its parameter tuning. As a result, you will realize that there is an exposure of mean decrease impurity, especially on these libraries. However, all these have serious problems, especially when you are dealing with data interpretation. In that, in correlated features, chances of getting low scores with stronger features are high. Due to this, you end up having affected by issues of biasedness towards variables comprising of several categories. Nevertheless, you can keep all these critical issues in your mind and use this method on your data.

It is also good to note that sometimes, the predicted outcome might have some errors and less accurate. However, there are several ways we can always use to improve our outcome. The first one involves fine-tuning of the used parameters within the algorithm. In this case, the vital parameters include the split features, the tree depth and also the total number of the trees.

Chapter 11: Perceptron Algorithm

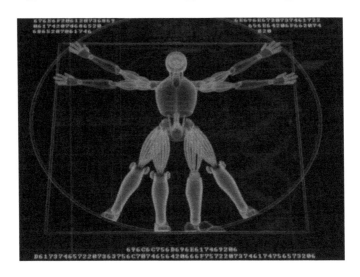

In this chapter, I have taken a look at the perceptron algorithm, defined it, and went on to illustrate how it works. In so doing, I have refreshed your minds on the necessary components of linear algebra before proceeding to study the perceptron learning algorithm. This step by step presentation is meant to guide learners in understanding and visualizing the concept of machine learning, taking note of the perceptron. It is my wish that by the end of the chapter, you have gained insight and knowledge to get you started. Additional materials of study are recommended.

Limitations and Precautionary Measures

In the training phase of the system, the perceptron algorithm should be helped to learn from acclimating data. This is to ensure that the prediction is accurate and errors barred. The presentation of input vector should reflect a due-diligent process. This ensures that the perceptron is set at par with the metrics and that the system can self-correct in case of errors as it just goes back to the provided input vector. The recommendation here is to ensure that any problem that needs solving through a linear separation has solved a set go based on the learning process. Another method to induce learning to the algorithm is by the use of a functioning train. This method set up networks within the algorithm and then produces input vectors to the perceptron. Afterward, the setup can correct the system depending on the number of errors to be fixed. Unfortunately, this method is faced by the uncertainty of convergence. There are no precise ways that can lead to convergence in the perceptron. For this reason, it is not advisable to use the function train method in training perceptron.

Despite the hype surrounding the use of perceptron learning algorithms, they do not fall short of limitations. The first limitation is that the output result in a perceptron network can only assume either a zero (0) or one (1) value. There are no in-between values. This can be seen as a biased outcome or an inaccurate one because sometimes we expect other values. The second drawback of the perceptron is that it can only be used to solve problems that require linear distinction. This implies that perceptron is only capable of working out issues that involve vectors that can be separated by a vertical plane. If a straight line cannot separate the vectors, then learning them becomes a hutch for the perceptron network. It is, however, worth noting that experts have proof to show that for linear separable quantities, perceptron learning algorithms can solve them in no time.

Perceptron may portray limitations. However, it is fair to note that a combination of networks (having numerous perceptron can be applied in complex problem-solving. For instance, say we have a unit of four problems to solve (four-vectors) by separating them with a straight line. In the process that we have two perceptrons in the network, it will create a two-dimension boundary that splits the vectors into four different groups.

Conclusion

An algorithm is a system that gives solutions and answers to question on a step by step basis. In computer science, algorithms provide results to search questions, offers recommendations on contents in accordance with the history of the user. Additionally, algorithms pool a large set of data to detect sequences and make forecasts about the habits of the user.

Algorithms can also be used to underpin prevailing partialities, particularly on digital media. For instance, double-tapping an online editorial that an acquaintance displayed on Instagram, which portrays political opinion, would show the Instagram algorithm that you have an interest in the political opinion posted. In the forthcoming, Instagram may set up your feeds to include the impression liked and filter out conventional feeds and views.

As a vital component of Python Machine Learning, the knowledge of algorithm involves; identifying the personal partialities in computer software design; analytically assessing the information available in the internet, and taking in to account the fact that the best news is always ranked first in the search results. All these are drawn from the digital media perspective. However, the knowledge of algorithms stretches far than just the digital media arena.

Almost every sector of the economy is applying the techniques of machine learning in day-to-day activities. The knowledge of python machine learning algorithms thereby becomes an essential tool for tackling dynamic problems in the real world.

Though not entirely looked at in this book, the question that draws debate is whether machine learning algorithms have a political character. As suggested by Tarleton Gillespie, it is vital to cross-examine the rationalities of premeditated populaces, by understanding the scope of influence of the digital tools and how the use of python machine learning algorithms have impacted our knowledge and if it may have political consequences.

The usefulness of agonistic nature in terms of machine learning may widen our understanding in areas where neural networks are structured. This broad understanding draws the conclusion that people make intelligent machines, and they are in fluidity and rooted infused places. Therefore, it essential to view the areas where the models are built as productive spots of research.

As discussed above, machine learning algorithms have become a significant part of our interactions and activities both in the social media and socio-economic platforms. And to answer the question of "can algorithms be agonistic?" It is crucial to take a look at past instances where algorithms have been considered to be combative. A good example was when the ML algorithms of Reddit provided a platform for most upvoted articles to be on top of search results thus promoting the spread of fake news at the time of the Boston Bombing in 2013.

As a result, a missing student, Sunil Tripathi, was mistakenly accused of carrying out the attacks.

Nowadays, almost all technical skills are influenced by the transformational model brought forth by the introduction of machine learning. This fact does not change the truth that the essential natural and human resources are limited. Therefore, the incorporation on intelligent machines in social activities should be done with precautionary measures taken to alleviate any potential risk.

Progressive procedures of machine learning may be useful in guiding the industrial processes towards an ideal way out. The methods, however, should not be programmed to find solutions to the same optimization problems in the same ways. A torrent of new sets of data and information is necessary to help this course. In the same spirit, developers and users of the software with algorithms of neural network should continue the innovative processes and research to find the ideal fit for every problem. This book is structured to guide my readers, among them with the necessary knowledge of python machine learning and relevant algorithms. It is hence essential to find additional sources to enhance the skills already acquired from this book.

Notes

www.ingramcontent.com/pod-product-compliance
Lightning Source LLC
Chambersburg PA
CBHW070840070326
40690CB00009B/1635